The
DEATH of
MEANING

Rousas John Rushdoony

**ROSS
HOUSE
BOOKS**

Vallecito, California

Ross House Books
PO Box 67
Vallecito, CA 95251

Library of Congress Control Number: 2002091738
ISBN: 1-879998-30-0

Printed in the United States of America

**Our thanks to those who made
the printing of this book possible**

Mr. & Mrs. Donald Alexander * Paul T. Bergaus * Clara Bianchi *
Michael & Marian Bowman * James & Judith Bruner *
John & Gloria Buzard * Dennis Clarys * Stephen & Janet Coakley *
Robert & Martha Coie * Kenneth W. Cope *
In Memory of Daniel Oliver Crews *
Richard & Elizabeth Crews * Jon & Patricia Davidson *
Dr. Anne L. Davis * David & Joan Dobert * Justin & Melanie Dock *
Dominion Covenant Church * Colonel & Miriam Doner *
In memory of Louise E. Duntz * John & Joan Dyer *
Rev. Dale Dykema & Reformation Presbyterian Church *
Dr. & Mrs. Nicholas H. Edwards * David & Maurietta Estler *
Harry & Marcella Fagan * Jack R. Faris * Robert & Marisa Frank *
Freedom Baptist Church *Michael & Mary Ann Frodella *
The Craig George Family * Dwight & Kathleen George *
Raphael A. Hanson III * Cathy Harnish * Keith & Antha Harnish *
Rev. & Mrs. Samuel D. Harrison * John William Helm *
William & Ruth Hewson * Dr. & Mrs. Herbert Hopper *
E.L.D.H. in memory of Lee & Thomas * Kenneth & Cindy Ii *
Earl & Dorothea Keener * Douglas Floyd Kelly * John B. King, Jr. *
David & Annie Knowles * Sarah Paris Kraft * Dr. & Mrs. Gary Kunsman *
John & Karen La Fear * Marguerite A. Lane * Dr. & Mrs. J.H. Lawson *
Gary Livingston * In memory of Muril & Florence Lovelace *
Joanna, Rachel & Daniel Manesajian * Steve & Belle Merritt *
Norman Milbank * Clint & Elizabeth Miller * Charles & Alfreida Moore *
Dr. Dean Moore * Timothy Patrick Murray * The Jim Nelson Family *
Dr. Heriberto Ortega * Chris & Anne Passerello *
The Howard Phillips Family * Gavin & Rachel Quill *
Greg Reger & Family * Steven Rogers * Frederic Rothfus *
Levi A. R. Rouse * Rebecca, Jill & Emily Rouse * April Rushdoony *
Terry & Janie Saxon * Virginia Schlueter * Anthony Schwartz *
Ford & Andrea Schwartz * Martin & Darlene Selbrede *
Guy Shea * Keith Shepherd *
SonRise Christian Community Church & Academy *
Phil & Petiflor Speilman * Eileen Stanley * Elmer & Naomi Stolzfus *
Martin Stroub * Scot Sullivan * Steve & Jacque Tanner *
Dr. David & Dorothy Terhune * Don & Betty Thompson *
Harry & Jo Ellen Valentine * Ellen Van Buskirk * Ellen Vasbinder *
Magnus Verbrugge * The Howard Walter Family *
Billie Welch * The Jeff White Family * Allan & Margaret Withington *
Roy S. Wright * David E. Young * Jeff & Cynthia Zylstra

Other books by
Rousas John Rushdoony

The Institutes of Biblical Law, Vol. I
The Institutes of Biblical Law, Vol. II, Law & Society
The Institutes of Biblical Law, Vol. III, The Intent of the Law
Systematic Theology (2 volumes)
Hebrews, James & Jude
The Gospel of John
Romans & Galatians
Thy Kingdom Come
This Independent Republic
The Nature of the American System
Foundations of Social Order
The "Atheism" of the Early Church
The Biblical Philosophy of History
The Mythology of Science
The Messianic Character of American Education
The Philosophy of the Christian Curriculum
Christianity and the State
Salvation and Godly Rule
God's Plan for Victory
Politics of Guilt and Pity
Roots of Reconstruction
The One and the Many
Revolt Against Maturity
By What Standard?
Law & Liberty

For a complete listing of available books
by Rousas John Rushdoony and other
Christian reconstructionists, contact:

ROSS HOUSE BOOKS
PO Box 67
Vallecito, CA 95251
www.rosshousebooks.org

Table of Contents

THE SOCIAL IMPLICATIONS OF DARWINISM

Foreword

Rousas John Rushdoony

The Death of Meaning gives the text of three different lecture series, delivered in different parts of the country, to illustrate the collapse of meaning in the modern world, its roots in philosophy and scientific thought, and its implications for man today.

The text was written prior to the lecture series, but with specific audiences in mind. The written text was, however, prepared for a reading audience.

The Direction of Modern Philosophy

Descartes and Modern Philosophy: The Birth of Subjectivism

One of the cherished myths of the modern age is that there was a "Copernican Revolution" which shifted the attention of European man from a man-centered perspective to a broader, universe-oriented worldview. Man no longer saw himself, we are told, as the center of the universe, and the earth as that point around which all things revolved, but saw instead the sun as the center. Man ostensibly shrank in size. Freud saw Copernicus, Darwin, and himself as the three men who had dealt destructive blows to man's soul. According to the myth, the church bitterly attacked Copernicus. Thus, according to Andrew White's very influential work,

> Calvin took the lead, in his *Commentary on Genesis*, by condemning all who asserted that the earth is not at the center of the universe. He clinched the matter by the usual reference to the first verse of the ninety-third Psalm, and asked, "Who will venture to place the authority of Copernicus above that of the Holy Spirit?"[1]

Unfortunately, White did not check his sources: Calvin apparently never even heard of Copernicus and made no

---

[1.] Andrew D. White, *A History of the Warfare of Science with Theology in Christendom*, vol. I (New York: George Braziller, 1955), 127.

reference to him.[2] In fact, Calvin left the door open for theoretical freedom in astronomy by insisting, in his commentary on Psalm 136:7,

> The Holy Spirit had no intention to teach astronomy; and, in proposing instruction meant to be common to the simplest and most uneducated persons, he made use by Moses and the other Prophets of popular language, that none might shelter himself under the pretext of obscurity, as we will see men sometimes very readily pretend an incapacity to understand, when anything deep or recondite is submitted to their notice.[3]

Luther was critical but essentially disinterested in Copernicus, although a Lutheran minister supervised the printing of Copernicus's study and wrote the preface to it. Although Rome censured the book, it left the door open to better evidence on the subject.[4]

Copernicus's (1473-1543) theory was essentially a revision of Ptolemy, whose system Copernicus accepted, and was designed to simplify rather than to destroy the Ptolemaic conception. How much the so-called "Copernican Revolution" has been a deduction of scholars, rather than a fact of history, appears in Will Durant's account of it. Note that Durant requires us to believe that men reacted as he feels they should have done, and concludes by effectually negating his thesis by stating that "Only a small minority in any generation would recognize the implications"!

> When men stopped to ponder the implications of the new system they must have wondered at the assumption that the Creator of this immense and orderly cosmos had sent His Son to die on this middling planet. All the lovely poetry of Christianity seemed to "go up in smoke" (as Goethe was to put it) at the touch of the Polish clergyman. The heliocentric astronomy compelled men to reconceive

---

[2.] Edward Rosen, "Calvin's Attitude Toward Copernicus," *Journal of the History of Ideas* (July – September, 1960) 21:441.

[3.] John Calvin, *Commentary on the Book of Psalms*, vol. V (Grand Rapids, MI: William B. Eerdmans, 1949), 184f.

[4.] William Hine, "Copernican Astronomy and Biblical Interpretation," in *Christian Scholar's Review*, (1973): 3, no. 2, 134-149.

God in less provincial, less anthropomorphic terms; it gave theology the strongest challenge in the history of religion. Hence the Copernican revolution was far profounder than the Reformation; it made the differences between Catholic and Protestant dogmas seem trivial; it pointed beyond the Reformation to the Enlightenment, from Erasmus and Luther to Voltaire, and even beyond Voltaire to the pessimistic agnosticism of a nineteenth century that would add the Darwinian to the Copernican catastrophe. There was but one protection against such men, and that was that only a small minority in any generation would recognize the implications of their thought. The sun will "rise" and "set" when Copernicus has been forgotten.[5]

What Durant gives us is the humanist's view of how Christendom *should* have reacted, not an historical account of its reaction. The pre-Copernican universe was no smaller than the post-Copernican cosmos. The damage to faith came, not from Copernicus, but from the later mechanical models of the universe which did not *expand* the universe but rather *eliminated* mind from it and *narrowed* the cosmos to mere matter.

The most erroneous aspect of the myth is the assumption that, with Copernicus, modern man turned from a belief in a small world and an absorption with the salvation of his soul to a cosmic view, to a perspective which gave him a vast and open universe. Nothing could be further from the truth. The modern faith has seen instead a steady and radical limitation of man's perspective, so that now, instead of an expansive world and life view that encompasses eternity, man's vision is limited to the confines of his existence, to his own mind.

This subjectivism was not new. It was common to pagan antiquity and was an important undercurrent of medieval thought. Yates's study of Giordano Bruno is telling evidence of the Hermetic and occultist nature of this undercurrent, which came into power with the Renaissance.[6] It was a "birth"

---

5. Will Durant, *The Story of Civilization: Part VI, The Reformation* (New York: Simon and Schuster, 1957), 863.

6. Frances A. Yates, *Giordano Bruno and the Hermetic Tradition* (New York: Vintage Books, 1969).

only in the sense that it was now in existence as a commanding motive in Western civilization and was a rival to Christian faith. The various philosophers of the Renaissance gave exotic forms to this Hermetic tradition. In Descartes, the same faith appears, not derived from the occultist tradition but from a common concept of being, as the fountainhead of the new philosophical tradition.

Supposedly, the "Copernican Revolution" gave man a cosmic perspective. In reality, with Descartes, modern man began a retreat into the confines of the mind.

With Rene Descartes (1596-1650), philosophy took as its starting point the mind of man as both autonomous and ultimate. Cushman said of Descartes' starting point, "He demanded the same return to an uncorrupted nature for the understanding that Rousseau many years later demanded for the heart."[7] The Aristotelian primacy of the autonomous mind of man, and its freedom from the corruption of sin, now gained a new eminence and centrality. As Cushman added, "For Descartes reality is within the Self; and the next question before him is how to get out of the Self."[8] Moreover, for Descartes "[t]he existence of God is an implication of human consciousness."[9] The mind of man is normative; it is neither fallen nor corrupt.

Molnar, in an excellent and telling analysis of Hermetic philosophy and epistemology, has shown its coincidence with modern philosophy at a critical point, *i.e.*, the equation of knowledge and being. As Molnar points out:

> ... the Hermetics equate *knowledge* and *being*: we *know* to the extent that we *are*, and the fuller, the more total our being, the more complete is also our knowledge....
>
> It does not occur to the Hermetic that being may be both unlimited (for example, or rather, outside time) and transcendent, and that man is constitutionally limited. He

---

[7.] Herbert Ernest Cushman, *A Beginner's History of Philosophy*, vol. II (Boston: Houghton Mifflin, 1911), 70.
[8.] *Ibid.*, 72.
[9.] *Ibid.*, 75.

does not recognize being unless he has entirely absorbed it with his intellectual faculties and permeated it with his consciousness to the point of total coincidence. The ideal must, then, be the equivalence of being and consciousness, the divine man, both Being and Knowledge.[10]

This equivalence describes not only the Hermetics, but, as Molnar shows, modern philosophy as well. In Descartes, there was an obvious formal Catholic faith, but even more clearly this equation of knowledge and being. Descartes declared:

> But because in this case I wished to give myself entirely to the search after Truth, I thought that it was necessary for me to take an apparently opposite course, and to reject as absolutely false everything as to which I could imagine the least ground of doubt, in order to see if afterwards there remained anything in my belief that was entirely certain. Thus, because our senses sometimes deceive us, I wished to suppose that nothing is just as they cause us to imagine it to be; and because there are men who deceive themselves in their reasoning and fall into paralogisms, even concerning the simplest matters of geometry, and judging that I was as subject to error as was any other, I rejected as false all the reasons formerly accepted by me as demonstrations. And since all the same thoughts and conceptions which we have while awake may also come to us in sleep, without any of them being at that time true, I resolved to assume that everything that ever entered into my mind was no more true than the illusions of my dreams. But immediately afterwards I noticed that whilst I thus wished to think all things false, it was absolutely essential that "I" who thought this should be somewhat, and remarking that this truth "*I think, therefore I am*" was so certain and so assured that all the most extravagant suppositions brought forward by the skeptics were incapable of shaking it, I came to the conclusion that I could receive it without scruple as the first principle of the Philosophy for which I was seeking.[11]

[10.] Thomas Molnar, *God and the Knowledge of Reality* (New York: Basic Books, 1973), 93.

[11.] Rene Descartes, *Discourse on the Method of Rightly Conducting the Reason and Seeking for Truth in the Sciences* (1637), Part 4, para. 1.

The main stream of philosophy had previously centered on God, either as the key problem or question, or, as with St. Anselm, as the starting point of all knowledge. In Descartes, philosophy began to eliminate this concern. *First* of all, Descartes's concern is for knowledge or truth as such, truth as something separate from God and not necessarily related to God. Later on, to eliminate his epistemological problem of contact between two alien substances, mind and the world of matter, Descartes posited a third factor, God, to insure their unity and the possibility of knowledge. God is thus a limiting concept, not the ground of truth but a connecting rod in the epistemological process between mind and the world of matter. Truth was separated from God, with far-reaching consequences. Truth was now something in the mind of man, a correspondence between the mind and the world. But, even more, the primary truth, "the first principle" of philosophy, was now, "I think, therefore I am." Not even the physical universe enters into this first principle, let alone God. The mind of man reigns alone, autonomous, and supreme in this first principle.

Second, while Descartes is a rationalist, his was a "scientific" rationalism which looked to mathematics for its guidance and inspiration. Now mathematics is a science of abstraction: it eliminates the concreteness of life, and life itself, to concentrate on one factor abstracted from reality, the numerical element. The more nearly "abstract" the reality approached, the more usable is mathematics; the more concrete and alive the reality, the less tenable mathematics becomes. To illustrate: two plus two equals four is a fact readily conceded, as long as it remains abstract. The matter is altered if we ask, are two boards of 12" x 16' equal to four boards of 6" x 16'? If our need is specifically for planks 12" wide, they are not the same; they are not equal. If four planks can be used equally as well as two, then they are more or less the same and equal. However, if we turn to life, the equation disappears into meaninglessness: are any two Englishmen and two Africans equal to any four Australians? Now we are in the world of people: the men can be of varying characters and intelligence, and these factors are not amenable to mathematical description. In brief, the mathematical model, when applied to life, to people, breaks down. Beginning with Descartes, modern philosophy has applied the mathematical model to reality, to the extent that it has recognized the outer world, and the outcome is an abstraction. The result has been a mechanical view of the universe. Life has been termed an epiphenomenon, not a reality. After Darwin, the mechanical model was replaced with an ostensibly biological model, but it is a biological model born of Descartes and Newton: the universe is a product of the void and has developed by chance and has neither mind nor teleology. But how can teleology be separated from biology? The problem is not solved by calling the teleology (in animals) "instinct"; it is merely evaded, because no explanation is given for the meaning of instinct. Like God in orthodox Christianity, instinct is a presupposition of modern biology, not a known and explicable fact.

In John Locke (1632-1704), the retreat of man from an objective universe took a further step inward. In *An Essay Concerning Human Understanding* (1690), Locke set forth the basic premises of the Enlightenment. Earlier, *An Essay on Toleration* (1667) had appeared, and, in 1695, *The Reasonableness of Christianity* was published; in these, the priority of the state and politics to religion and the church was assumed, and Deism was granted a respectable beginning. Although known as the father of British empiricism, Locke's perspective in religion was strictly rationalistic. Thus, *first*, we find in Locke an assertion of the priority of reason over religion and God, so that what is recognized as true is that which is declared to be rational. Although Locke's conclusions concerning Christianity were conservative, and reflected his Puritan parentage, his presuppositions were radical. Reason assumes ultimacy and becomes the judge and arbiter over all reality. An orthodox Christian, because he believes in the sovereignty and omniscience of God, holds that all reality is rational, in that all reality is a creation of the totally self-

conscious and purposive God; he will recognize that his
created reason is not able to comprehend the totality of God
and of His creation, but he will at the same time recognize it as
comprehensible. In brief, there are no brute facts, no
meaningless facts, in the universe. All have their meaning,
although only God's mind can grasp the totality of His
creation. In contrast, the non-Christian thinker denies in
principle the total meaning and rationality of the cosmos,
because he denies that it is the unified work of the sovereign
God; in consequence, he insists on the ultimacy of his own
mind and its ability to recognize what element of meaning
there may be, and he imposes his own meaning upon reality.

Locke set out to prove why the Bible had to be believed, and
why it was given as a revelation. In prior ages, he pointed out,
none, however reasonable at times, followed systematically
the laws of Reason. As a result, the Bible had been directed to
the darkness of men's minds.

> 'Tis not every Writer of Morals, or Compiler of it from
> others, that can thereby be erected into a Law-giver to
> Mankind; and a Dictator of Rules, which are therefore
> valid, because they are found in his Books; under the
> authority of this or that Philosopher. He that any one will
> pretend to set up in this kind, and have his Rules to pass
> for authentick Directions, must shew, that either he builds
> his Doctrine upon Principles of Reason, self-evident in
> themselves; and that he deduces all the parts of it from
> thence, by clear and evident Demonstration; Or must
> shew his Commission from Heaven, that he comes with
> Authority from God, to deliver his Will and Commands
> to the World.
>
> In the former way, no body that I know before our
> Saviour's time, ever did, or went about to give us a
> Morality. 'Tis true there is a Law of Nature; but who is
> there that ever did, or undertook to give it us all entire, as
> a Law; no more, nor no less, than what was contained in,
> and had the Obligation of that Law? Who ever made out
> all the parts of it, put them together, and shewed the
> World their Obligation?[12]

Now, finally, the Law of Nature was being systematically studied, and the implicit assumption, which the Deists pursued, was that now a rational religion and morality were possible, and the old paraphernalia and guises of authority could be dropped for the authority of Reason. The age of "self-evident" truth had arrived. According to Cushman, the Deists, who sought to free religion and the idea of law from dogma, had certain presuppositions:

> Deism was founded on three principles: (1) the origin of religion may be scientifically investigated; (2) the origin of religion is in the conscience; (3) positive religions are degenerate forms of natural religion.... Deism was quite consistent with the central principle of this period—the self-sufficiency of the individual.[13]

Religion, moreover, became a matter of opinion, and belief in God a personal option. At the beginning of *A Letter Concerning Toleration,* Locke spoke with horror of "the burning zeal" of churchmen which had led to literal burnings "with fire and faggot." This he saw as clearly wrong. It did not occur to him to say also that civil government, in hanging and beheading men for treason, might also be wrong. For the Enlightenment and modern man, religious order is optional and dispensable; political order is not. The more religious order has been dropped, as in National Socialist and Marxist countries, the more rigid has the civil order become, and the more active the executioners. Modern man has not abolished intolerance or persecution. He holds, with more fervor than the Inquisitors, that what is worth believing is worth executing and killing for: he has merely shifted his faith from the church to the state. Locke defined the church in *A Letter Concerning Toleration* as "a free and voluntary society." The state was for him the necessary society, and hence a compulsive and coercive society. Religion was now well on the road, together with God, to being reduced to *opinion,* whereas Reason was now allied with the state and politics. As a consequence,

---

[12.] John Locke, *The Reasonableness of Christianity.*

[13.] Cushman, *op. cit.,* 2, 165.

although Deism worked towards a *rational* religion, the Enlightenment as a whole preferred the *abolition* of religion and the establishment of a *rational* state. As a result also, a major area of activity for philosophic thought was the creation of rational models for civil reform. Monarchy was thus increasingly in disfavor, and ideas for the recreation of civil government in terms of philosopher-kings or elite intellectuals began to abound. Reality had to become what the mind willed it to be, not what history, tradition, or property rights had made it. Locke thus wrote his essays *Concerning the True Original Extent and End of Civil Government.* This Enlightenment concern was to establish the "state of Nature" and its consequences for man, but the state of Nature is at this point still a correlative of Right Reason. When conflict between the state of Nature and Reason later appeared, it was Reason, all along the implicit ultimate, which triumphed. Nature, the objective universe, was reduced to an aspect of the experience of man's mind.

Second, Locke's philosophy, associational in nature, presupposed the mind as a blank, white piece of paper, *i.e.,* clean, clear, and impartial, untainted by presuppositions and *a priori* ideas. Such an assumption was necessary to the ultimacy of the mind: it preserved the integrity of the mind as the impartial arbiter of reality. Right Reason had validity because it was untainted. Thus, behind the empiricism of Locke stands a full-fledged rationalism. Empiricism is the *methodology* of some forms of rationalism, not a competing philosophy. The quarrel between idealism and empiricism is a methodological quarrel between various forms of rationalism. For Locke, the mind is free; it begins without prejudice and without any claims against it.

Third, Locke's epistemology has the Cartesian background of dualism, the dualism of mind and matter. This dualism is one that all modern thought struggles with, and attempts to overcome.[14] It is important to recognize the meaning of this

---

[14.] See R.J. Rushdoony, *The One and the Many* (Nutley, NJ: The Craig Press, 1971).

problem. It is true that it is inherited from Greek philosophy, but why did this problem bedevil Greek and Oriental philosophies, and why does it continue to trouble modern thought as well? The problem comes from the fact that, if something is ultimate in the universe, *i.e.*, whatever is the starting point and presupposition of a faith or a philosophy, then all else is derivative and/or secondary, and a dualism results. In Biblical faith, this dichotomy is between Creator and creation or creature. Where God is denied, another dichotomy results. In modern thought, as much as in ancient philosophy, this dichotomy is between the autonomous and ultimate mind of man and the universe. In some forms, the universe is reduced to illusion, and only the mind of man exists, soon itself to become nothingness. In other forms, as in the West after Kant, the dichotomy is resolved by absorbing the universe into the mind and/or experience of man.

Thus, while modern philosophy is subjective, and is a progressively intensive retreat into the autonomous mind of man, the purpose of this retreat is the conquest of the world by means of the supposed Archimedean point or lever, the mind of man. The unquestioned reality is the mind of man; the problematical reality and/or illusion is the material universe, and also God.

Locke hoped to tie the mind to the universe by means of association, the association of sensations of the outer world with the mind, an untainted and pure mind which passively receives sense impressions of outer reality. Problems immediately arose with regard to the validity of the report of sense impressions. Bishop George Berkeley (1685-1753) "solved" the problem by reducing Descartes' trichotomy of mind, matter, and God to a dichotomy of mind and God. In *A Treatise Concerning the Principles of Human Knowledge* (Introduction, 3), Berkeley declared:

> That neither our thoughts, nor passions, nor ideas formed by the imagination, exist without the mind, is what every body will allow. And it seems no less evident that the various sensations or ideas imprinted on the sense,

however blended or combined together (that is, whatever objects they compose), cannot exist otherwise than in a mind perceiving them. I think an intuitive knowledge may be obtained of this, by any one that shall attend to what is meant by the term *exist*, when applied to sensible things. The table I write on, I say, exists, that is, I see and feel it: and if I were out of my study I should say it existed, meaning thereby that if I was in my study I might perceive it, or that some other spirit actually does perceive it. There was an odour, that is, it was smelled; there was a sound, that is to say, it was heard; a colour or figure, and it was perceived by sight or touch. This is all that I can understand by these and the like expressions. For as to what is said of the absolute existence of unthinking things without any relation to their being perceived, that seems perfectly unintelligible. There *esse* is *percipi*, nor is it possible that they should have any existence out of the minds or thinking things which perceive them.[15]

To be is to be perceived, or, more accurately, to be is to be perceived by the autonomous mind of man. The perceptions come from God, so that two substances alone exist, God and man. God sends the ideas to man's mind, so that the entire sensible universe is an orderly perception "existed" by God. As Berkeley declared,

> The ideas imprinted on the senses by the Author of nature are called *real things*: and those excited in the imagination being less regular, vivid and constant, are more properly termed *ideas* or *images of things*, which they copy and represent. But then our sensations, be they never so vivid and distinct, are nevertheless *ideas*, that is, they exist in the mind, or are perceived by it, as truly as the ideas of its own framing. The ideas of the sense are allowed to have more reality in them, that is, to be more strong, orderly, and coherent than the creatures of the mind; but this is no argument that they exist without the mind.[16]

For Berkeley, God was a sufficient explanation for the natural order; the natural order is simply a vast complex of ideas which

---

[15.] *The Works of George Berkeley*, vol. I (London: Richard Priestly, 1820), 24.

[16.] *Ibid.*, 38f.

are excited in us by God, and it has no being in itself. The proof of the existence of God for Berkeley was precisely this vast complex of sensations and ideas which we call the universe. "Everything we see, hear, feel, or anywise perceive by sense being a sign or effect of the power of God," it follows that "we do at all times and in all places perceive manifest tokens of the Divinity."[17] Thus,

> It is therefore plain, that nothing can be more evident to any one that is capable of the least reflection, than the existence of God, or a spirit who is intimately present in our minds, producing in them all that variety of ideas or sensations, which continually affect us, on whom we have an absolute and entire dependence, in short, "in whom we live, and move, and have our being." That the discovery of this great truth which lies so near and obvious to the mind, should be attained to by the reason of so very few, is a sad instance of the stupidity and inattention of men, who, though they are surrounded with such clear mani-festations of the Deity, are yet so little affected by them, that they seem as it were blinded with excess of light.[18]

Unfortunately for Berkeley, Occam's razor soon went to work on his thesis, *i.e.*, the logical implications were followed to reduce man to his mind. If to be is to be perceived by the mind of man, then what being does Berkeley's god have? Has autonomous man *perceived* God? Is God an object in sense impressions? It clearly followed that David Hume (1711-1776) was able to eliminate *both* God and the universe: man has no direct experience of either; all man has are sense impressions, or ideas about sense impressions, and thus all that can be said to exist is the mind. Immanuel Kant (1724-1804) tried to rescue knowledge by restoring Descartes' trichotomy on a new basis: the subjective mind of man, phenomena, and things-in-themselves. The realm of knowledge is phenomena, but "reality," things-in-themselves, is not knowable. We assume the existence of things-in-themselves, whether of God or of

---

[17.] *Ibid.*, 101.
[18.] *Ibid.*

our own subjective states of mind, and the phenomena which appear in our subjective states as an aspect of our experience.

One result of this was the radical separation of faith and reason. What the naïve experience of man had regarded as the real world, and the sovereign Creator thereof, now became the realm of faith and was thus inaccessible to reason. Again, what naïve experience had previously regarded as a hindrance to valid knowledge, namely, the subjective states of man's mind, now became the area of reason, knowledge, and science. The inability of most people to grasp this violation of naïve experience is the reason for their failure to recognize the full radical import of modern philosophy.

Hume saw the world and the God of naïve experience as projections of man's mind. Berkeley had seen the material world as a creation of ideas excited in our minds by God. Hume and Kant in effect reversed this concept, and Schopenhauer called the world our will and idea. In his *Natural History of Religion*, Hume traced the evolution of religion and theology in terms of this projection.

> There is an universal tendency among mankind to conceive all beings like themselves, and to transfer to every object those qualities with which they are familiarly acquainted, and of which they are intimately conscious.... The *unknown causes* which continually employ their thought, appearing always in the same aspect, are all apprehended to be of the same kind or species. Nor is it long before we ascribe to them thought, and reason, and passion, and sometimes even the limbs and figures of men, in order to bring them nearer to a resemblance with ourselves.[19]

Life, order, meaning, and objective reality were being withdrawn from the world outside of man. The only truly knowable world was in the confines of man's mind.

[19.] Professor (sic) Huxley, *Hume* (London: Macmillan, 1881), 158.

2

Berkeley to Kant:
The Collapse of the Outer World

It is necessary at this point briefly to retrace some ground in order to summarize the effect of modern philosophy on science. When Descartes divided reality into two alien substances, mind and body, held together by a third substance, God, he thereby deformed man's perspective on both mind and body. The mind increasingly was seen in neoplatonic terms as an alien and spiritual substance, so that the Biblical unity of man was lost. Attempts to locate the mind were rendered increasingly unscientific and irrelevant. At the same time, the body was reduced to a machine by Descartes, a mechanism without mind and subject to purely mechanical laws and to be understood in terms of them.[1]

Thomas Hobbes (1588-1679) challenged the validity of Descartes' dualism. He held that the only reality is matter in motion: sensation, thought, and consciousness were reduced to phantasms created by the actions of atoms in the brain. Hobbes's views were premature and did not find ready acceptance because of the suspicion of unbelief which clung to his name; but Sir Isaac Newton (1642-1727) had the odor of

---

[1.] Sir William Dampier, *A History of Science, and its Relations with Philosophy and Religion* (New York: Macmillan, 1944), 148f.

sanctity, whether or not deserved, and his reduction of the physical world to matter and motion, a mechanical principle explicable entirely in mathematical terms, did gain favor almost at once, to a far greater degree than Newton probably intended. In the Preface to the first edition of his *Mathematical Principles of Natural Philosophy* (1686), Newton wrote:

> I offer this work as the mathematical principles of philosophy, for the whole burden of philosophy seems to consist in this—from the phenomena of motions to investigate the other phenomena; and to this end the general propositions in the first and second book are directed. In the third book I give an example of this in the explication of the System of the World; for by the propositions mathematically demonstrated in the former books in the third I derive from the celestial phenomena the forces of gravity with which bodies tend to the sun and the several planets. Then from these forces, by other propositions which are also mathematical, I deduce the motions of the planets, the comets, the moon, and the sea. I wish we could derive the rest of the phenomena of Nature by the same kind of reasoning from mechanical principles, for I am induced by many reasons to suspect that they may all depend on certain forces by which the particles of bodies, by some causes hitherto unknown, are either mutually impelled towards one another, and cohere in regular figures, or are repelled and recede from one another. These forces being unknown, philosophers have hitherto attempted the search of Nature in vain; but I hope the principles here laid down will afford some light either to this or some truer method of philosophy.[2]

Bishop Berkeley accepted the Newtonian view, but asked the further question as to which was the real world, the world of the mind with its mathematical principles, or the empty, dead world of matter? He did not deny the testimony of sense impressions or experience. Rather, Berkeley confined knowledge to this world of thought or sense impressions. Thus, in the third of his *Three Dialogues Between Hylas and*

---

2. Isaac Newton, *Mathematical Principles of Natural Philosophy* (Chicago: Encyclopedia Britannica, 1952), preface, 1f.

Philonous, In Opposition to Sceptics and Atheists, Philonous declares:

> With all my heart: retain the word *matter*, and apply it to the objects of sense, if you please, provided you do not attribute to them any subsistence distinct from their being perceived. I shall never quarrel with you for an expression. *Matter,* or *material substance,* are terms introduced by philosophers; and as used by them, imply a sort of independency, or a subsistence distinct from being perceived by a mind: but are never used by common people; or, if ever, it is to signify the immediate objects of sense. One would think, therefore, so long as the names of all particular things, with the terms *sensible, body, stuff,* and the like, are retained, the word *matter* should never be missed in common talk. And in philosophical discourses it seems the best way to leave it quite out; since there is not, perhaps, any one thing that hath more favoured and strengthened the depraved bent of the mind towards atheism, than the use of that general confused term.[3]

In *An Essay Towards a New Theory of Vision,* Berkeley stressed the fact that all we really see are sensations, not the material world itself. In the *Principles of Human Knowledge,* Berkeley asserted that all that exists is our knowledge. In the first sentence of this latter treatise, Berkeley declared:

> It is evident to any one who takes a survey of the objects of human knowledge, that they are either ideas actually imprinted on the senses, or else such as are perceived by attending to the passions and operations of the mind, or lastly, ideas formed by help of memory and imagination, either compounding, dividing, or barely representing, those originally perceived in the aforesaid ways.[4]

Very clearly, Berkeley began with a commitment to the empiricism of Locke. Moreover, with Descartes, Locke, and all of modern philosophy, Berkeley, for all his piety, began with the assumption or presupposition of the ultimacy and autonomy of the mind of man. Berkeley was thus a world

---

[3.] *The Works of George Berkeley,* vol. I (London: Richard Priestly, 1820), 222.
[4.] *Ibid.,* vol. 1, 23.

removed from the ordinary believer of a century before, whose faith was a world and life view. Berkeley's religion, philosophy, and science had retreated into the mind of man. In religion, the consequence was soon to become manifest in pietism and experientialism (or, as it was then called, experimental religion).

Berkeley claimed to present a "common sense" philosophy, without unwarranted assumptions. In one sense, he was right. The lifeless, mechanistic, material universe of Newton (after Descartes) was *not* the world of common sense. It was, in time, to become the world of modern man, cold, empty, silent, and dead; but the "common sense" of Berkeley's day did not accept it. It was the Enlightenment thinkers who welcomed it as liberation from God. Joseph Addison, as a rationalist and a party to the new intellectualism, wrote his famous ode to answer the "common sense" distaste for the new view of things, and to insist that the Deist's god made all this emptiness and silence wonderful to Reason, because the universe's mathematical order sang more gloriously than its silence:

> What though, in solemn silence, all
> Move round the dark terrestrial ball?
> What tho' nor real voice nor sound
> Amid their radiant orbs be found?
>
> In reason's ear they all rejoice,
> And utter forth a glorious voice,
> For ever singing as they shine,
> "The hand that made us is divine."

This is the cold world of Newton, that Berkeley's "common sense" philosophy and his empiricism undercut. For him, apart from God, minds and ideas are all that exist. His presupposition is the mind, and Hume, operating on the same Cartesian presupposition, reduced philosophy to the contents of the mind: ideas.

For Berkeley, all things are simply perceptions. All ideas, both perceptions and images, are passive. Here Berkeley followed the implicit passivity of the mind which is common to Descartes and Locke. For both of these men, the veracity of knowledge in part depended on this passive character of the mind. The mind is the receiver, neutral and clean of bias, so that it faithfully records what the senses report. Add "Right Reason," *i.e.*, clear and rigorous induction and deduction, to the senses, and you have true knowledge. Empiricists like Locke were thus intensely concerned with establishing "Right Reason" as the necessary receiver of faithful impressions. For Berkeley, the *active* agents in ideas are, first, God, who sends the impressions which the mind receives, and, second, the spirit, which is the true man.

Hume cannot be appreciated apart from his admiration for Berkeley; Hume's work was clearly based on Berkeley's premises. He insisted that we can only know ideas, and ideas are the only existences we know. To assume God and soul or spirit is as invalid as to assume a material universe.

Moreover, in Section 7, "Of the Idea of Necessary Connection," of *An Inquiry Concerning Human Understanding*, Hume attacked the concept of causality as of psychological rather than natural origin. The world of Newton, being a mechanical world, requires association by contiguity to produce results. If a billiard ball moves, it is because another billiard ball, for example, has struck it. In the Newtonian world, God was necessary as a first cause, as the starter of the action. As a result of this, Hume said, "according to these philosophers, everything is full of God."[5] This line of reasoning, said Hume, gets us "into fairyland."[6]

It appears, then, that this idea of a necessary connection among events arises from a number of similar instances which occur, of the constant conjunction of these events; nor can that idea ever be suggested by any one of these instances surveyed in all possible lights and positions. But there is nothing in a number of instances, different from every single instance, which is supposed to be exactly similar, except only that after a repetition of similar instances the mind is carried by habit, upon the

---

[5] David Hume, *An Inquiry Concerning Human Understanding* (New York: The Liberal Arts Press, 1955), 82.
[6] *Ibid.*, 83.

appearance of one event, to expect its usual attendant and to believe that it will exist. This connection, therefore, which we *feel* in the mind, this customary transition of the imagination from one object to its usual attendant, is the sentiment or impression from which we form the idea of power or necessary connection. Nothing further is in the case. Contemplate the subjects on all sides, you will never find any other origin of that idea. This is the sole difference between one instance, from which we can never receive the idea connection, and a number of similar instances by which it is suggested. The first time a man saw the communication of motion by impulse, as by the shock of two billiard balls, he could not pronounce that the one event was *connected*, but only that is was *conjoined* with the other. After he has observed several instances of this nature, he then pronounces them to be *connected*. What alteration has happened to give rise to this new idea of *connection?* Nothing but that he now *feels* these events to be *connected* in his imagination, and can readily foretell the existence of one from the appearance of the other. When we say, therefore, that one object is connected with another, we mean only that they have acquired a connection in our thought and gave rise to this inference by which they become proofs of each other's existence – a conclusion which is somewhat extraordinary, but which seems founded on sufficient evidence. Nor will its evidence be weakened by any general difference of the understanding or skeptical suspicion concerning every conclusion which is new and extraordinary. No conclusions can be more agreeable to skepticism than such as make discoveries concerning the weakness and narrow limits of human reason and capacity.[7]

Given the premises of modern philosophy, Hume's conclusions are valid. The only possible valid knowledge becomes *exhaustive* knowledge; if we know every connection of two kinds of events from the beginning to the end of time, then we can come to valid and assured knowledge. We must add, however, that with the modern view of infinite time, this impossible ideal is rendered doubly impossible. For Hume, all that we can truly know are our *ideas*, nothing more. Hume did

---

7. *Ibid.*, 86f.

not deny that the physical universe exists; he denied that it could be known. To a limited degree, some idea of the world was possible for Hume by means of mathematics, dealing with number and quantity, and by means of experimental reasoning, but all this could lead only, to use more modern terms, to a practical and pragmatic truth, not to any historically held idea of absolute or assured truth. In the well-known words of the conclusion of his *Inquiry*, Hume declared,

> When we run over libraries, persuaded of these principles, what havoc must we make? If we take in our hand any volume—let us ask, *Does it contain any abstract reasoning concerning quantity or number?* No. *Does is contain any experimental reasoning concerning matter of fact and existence?* No. Commit it then to the flames, for it can contain nothing but sophistry and illusion.[8]

Reasoning had to be *abstract* because now only an abstract universe existed for modern philosophy, a universe from which God, mind, life, meaning, sound, and all else save quantity and number had been extracted. A new "common sense" view of "nature" was now in the making, a dead universe in which man is an accident looking hopefully at the stars in the hope that somewhere the accident of life and mind has occurred on another planet.

How does man live in Hume's universe? Not by total skepticism, Hume held, but by a practical acceptance of a world he must theoretically negate. In the conclusion to Book 1 of his *Treatise on Human Nature*, Hume wrote:

> Shall we then establish it for a general maxim, that no refined or elaborate reasoning is ever to be received? If we embrace this principle, we run into the most manifest absurdities. If we reject it in favor of those reasonings, we subvert entirely the human understanding. We have, therefore, no choice left, but between a false reason and none at all. Most fortunately it happens that since reason is incapable of dispelling these clouds, nature suffices to that purpose, and cures me of this philosophical

---

[8.] *Ibid.*, 173.

melancholy. I dine, I play a game of backgammon, I converse, and am merry with my friends.—No: If I must be a fool, as all who reason or believe anything certainly are, my follies shall at least be natural and agreeable. In all the incidents of life we ought still to preserve our skepticism. Where reason is lively and mixes itself with some propensity it ought to be assented to.

Hume's conclusion that causality is neither self-evident nor demonstrable was accepted by Immanuel Kant (1724-1804), who recognized that this same doubt is valid with respect to all other principles and fundamentals of science and philosophy. In effect all that remained in the world after Hume was ideas, pure reason. All else was open to radical doubt. The presupposition of Cartesian philosophy was the autonomous mind or reason of man. The logic of this premise, accepted by modern philosophy, left it with nothing but pure reason. For Hume, thought had no objective or metaphysical validity of any kind, although Leibniz tried to hold that it did. Kant agreed that universality and necessity (or causality) are not empirical deductions. They are rational synthesis, not an intrinsic necessity. The necessity of these things is to the human reason, not to the material world. They are conditions of our sense experience, not an aspect of things in themselves. Newtonian science deals with appearance, not reality. The world of science is the realm of phenomena, of appearance, not of things in themselves.

Thus, what in modern philosophy from Descartes through Hume was a problem and a limitation became in Kant a virtue. The retreat of the mind into itself, and the limitation of rationality to the mind, became, not problems to Kant, but rather the starting point of greater claims for the autonomous mind of man. Kant's thesis is summed up in three short sentences in his "Preface to the Second Edition" of his *Critique of Pure Reason*:

> Hitherto it has been assumed that all our knowledge must conform to objects. But all attempts to extend our knowledge of objects by establishing something in regard

to them *a priori*, by means of concepts, have, on this assumption, ended in failure. We must therefore make trial whether we may not have more success in the tasks of metaphysics, if we suppose that objects must conform to our knowledge.[9]

Moreover, in terms of this, Kant could declare that *"[t]he understanding does not derive its laws (a priori) for, but prescribes them to, nature."*[10]

Kant's world, like Descartes', is a trichotomy, but with a difference. Instead of mind, body, and God, we have in Kant subjective states, phenomena (the realm of knowledge), and things-in-themselves. Things-in-themselves are not knowable; they cannot even be called the world of material bodies or natural objects: the hard, cold, and dead world of Newton is gone, and the world of Hegel and Darwin is in its dawning, a world of phenomena in which the order is derived from mind, man's mind. The reality of noumena, things-in-themselves, is neither denied nor affirmed. They are limiting concepts: their role is not unlike that of the god of Deism, needed to avoid the problem of infinite regress but definitely kept out of the world after being posited as its starting point. So, too, things-in-themselves maintain a formal reference point for reality without being real. God, too, was to become a limiting concept in theology, and, in Paul Tillich, God is spoken of as one of whom it cannot be said that He exists or that He does not exist. He is "beyond" the category of existence and functions simply as a limiting concept for the reasonings of man's autonomous mind. What is real for the mind is its experience, the world of things-for-us, a reality relative to man. Absolute reality is not of any significance nor a matter of concern; rather, the emphasis, and the realm of knowledge, is the world of phenomena or experience, of reality relative to us, of things-for-us.

[9.] Norman Kemp Smith, translator, *Immanual Kant's Critique of Pure Reason* (London: Macmillan, 1934), 16.

[10.] Paul Carus, editor, *Kant's Prolegomena to Any Future Metaphysics* (La Salle, IL: Open Court, 1955), 82.

Down the road from this lies existentialism, and the hippie emphasis on "doing your own thing" as the truth for man. The principle of Kant is that *only in experience is there truth.*

In 1748, Julien Offray De La Mettrie published his Cartesian study, *Man A Machine.* Descartes had taught that animals are mere machines, an aspect of the dead material universe. La Mettrie reduced man to the same machine.[11] Now a new opinion had been introduced, or a variation of the Cartesian premise: man is an experiencing man. To live, the Romantic movement of the nineteenth and twentieth centuries was soon to say, is to experience, and the fervid quest for experience was under way. The reality of God and an outer world had been replaced by a new "reality" of experience.

[11.] Julien Offray De La Mettrie, *Man a Machine* (La Salle, IL: Open Court, 1943).

3

Hegel to Marx to Dewey:
The Creation of a New World

Modern philosophy had concluded that, since the world is beyond understanding, and because things-in-themselves, if they exist, are still unknowable, *first*, the only real world for autonomous man is himself, and, *second*, the "problem" of philosophy is no longer knowing and understanding the world, but remaking it in man's own image.

Auguste Comte (1798-1857) captured the spirit of modern philosophy in his formulation of Positivism. For him, the history of thought had three different theoretical conditions: first, the theological or fictitious era, during which men were governed by a belief in ultimate meaning that was thought to be discovered in religion. Second came the metaphysical or abstract condition, in which men still sought for meaning, although they did so rationally rather than religiously. In the third, the scientific or positive phase, men abandon the quest for absolute knowledge and meaning. Instead of seeking first and final causes and definitive truth, men now renounce all such efforts for a purely technological and utilitarian approach. *Method* becomes the main concern. Comte still believed in natural laws, so that he had not entirely cut his ties with truth in knowledge, but he clearly set forth an essentially methodological approach to knowledge. Not meaning but scientific workability became paramount.

The foundation for this approach was established by Georg Wilhelm Friedrich Hegel (1770-1831). In Hegel we have the façade of traditionalism. His philosophy is ostensibly concerned with God, called *Geist*, Mind or Spirit. This spirit, however, is not *beyond* history but *is* history, *man's history*. History is not God's act, an aspect of His creation and of the ordained processes thereof, but it is in Hegel *man's act*. Not God but Reason, man's reason, is "the Sovereign of the World" for Hegel. Hegel wrote:

> The only Thought which Philosophy brings with it to the contemplation of History, is the simple conception of *Reason*; that Reason is the Sovereign of the World; that the history of the world, therefore, presents us with a rational process. This conviction and intuition is a hypothesis in the domain of history as such. In that of Philosophy it is no hypothesis. It is there proved by speculative cognition, that Reason—and this term may here suffice us, without investigating the relation sustained by the Universe to the Divine Being—is *Substance*, as well as *Infinite Power*; its own *Infinite Material* underlying all the natural and spiritual life which it originates, as also the *Infinite Form*—that which sets the Material in motion. On the one hand, Reason is the *substance* of the Universe; *viz.* that by which and in which all reality has its being and subsistence. On the other hand, it is the *Infinite Energy* of the Universe; since Reason is not so powerless as to be incapable of producing anything but a mere ideal, a mere intention—having its place outside reality, nobody knows where; something separate and abstract, in the heads of certain human beings. It is *the infinite complex of things*, their entire Essence and Truth.[1]

Reason is the Divine in man.[2] The "essential *destiny* of Reason" is "identical with the question, *what is the ultimate design of the world?*"[3] "The perfect embodiment of Spirit" or Reason is "the

---

[1.] G.W.F. Hegel, *Philosophy of History* (New York: P.F. Collier & Son, 1901), 52f.

[2.] *Ibid.*, 81.

[3.] *Ibid.*, 60.

State."[4] Spirit, moreover, is autonomous and self-contained. It is unlike matter in this respect as in others, in that matter is governed by gravity, by a force outside of itself.

> Spirit, on the contrary, may be defined as that which has its centre in itself. It has not a unity outside itself, but has already found it; it exists *in* and *with itself.* Matter has its essence out of itself; Spirit is *self-contained existence....* Now this is Freedom, exactly. For if I am dependent, my being is referred to something else which I am not; I cannot exist independently of something external. I am free, on the contrary, when my existence depends on myself.[5]

The historic doctrine of the aseity or self-existence of God becomes in Hegel the doctrine of the aseity of man. Consequently, man is cut loose even from his matter, and the old hated Hellenic dualism returns as a necessary condition of man's autonomy. The ground, too, is clearly prepared for existentialism.

Moreover, for modern man *politics* is the key area of human activity. It is apparently or seemingly free from compelling external laws (such as gravity) and offers freedom for man to play god, to remake the world. The state is man's key to a rational recreation of man and the world. For Hegel, therefore, "[t]he State is the Divine Idea as it exists on Earth."[6] Since, however, the essence of Spirit or Reason is self-determination or absolute freedom, this means that when man's freedom is fully realized, the individual is a law unto himself.[7] The way was thus prepared by Hegel for both the idea of the state as the dictatorship of the proletariat, and the final stage of communism as anarchism, the perfection of Reason and Freedom in an autonomous and harmonious society in which all men, being the embodiments of reason, need no state, because the perfected state is now an automatic

---

4. *Ibid.*, 61.
5. *Ibid.*, 62.
6. *Ibid.*, 87.
7. *Ibid.*, 164.

and stateless communism, totally rational and scientific, and perfectly operative.

For Hegel, "[a]n existent of any sort embodying the free will, that is what right is. Right therefore is by definition freedom as Idea."[8] Because the state epitomizes the spirit of humanism in the modern era, "[t]he state is the actuality of the ethical Idea."[9]

With such an idea of freedom, it is not surprising that, in the nineteenth and twentieth centuries, both nationalism (the free self-determination of national states) and radical individualism and anarchism (the free self-determination of autonomous man) flourished. History was now god, and the key to power was self-determination, the command of history by men and nations. For modern college students, the *one* ethical idea is very commonly this Hegelian doctrine of freedom.

Karl Marx (1818-1883) was Hegelian to the core. His work was the application of Hegelianism to the economic scene. For Marx, *Geist* was now identified with material processes, with dialectical materialism, but it was still Reason. Marx's economics is a radical environmentalism in its implications and in its historical impact, but Marx still saw Reason as that aspect of the materialistic process which *determined* history. The third of his "Theses on Feuerbach" declared:

> The materialist doctrine that men are products of circumstances and upbringing, and that, therefore, changed men are products of other circumstances and upbringing, forgets that it is men that change circumstances and that the educator himself needs educating. Hence, this doctrine necessarily arrives at dividing the society into two parts, of which one is superior to society (in Robert Owen, for example).

---

8. G.W.F. Hegel, *The Philosophy of Right* (Chicago: Encyclopaedia Britannica, 1955), 19.
9. *Ibid.*, 80.

The coincidence of the changing of circumstances and of human activity can be conceived and rationally understood only as *revolutionizing practice.*[10]

Why this contradiction? The reason for it lies in the fact that the Biblical doctrine of sin and responsibility is denied. Man is not under God: in the world of modern philosophy, man is only responsible to himself. Man, then, as autonomous, will not confess to sin. Where then does the responsibility for his condition lie? It is projected on to the environment, to capitalism, parents, educators, church, and community. Guilt is thus passed on, but so is responsibility, and environmentalism prevails. Man, by seeking absolute freedom, ends up a conditioned product of his environment. Marx, a racial environmentalist, refused to see the plight in which he left man. He insisted on both economic determinism and Hegelian freedom. The goal of the new man, the new philosophy, was the control of history to remake man.

Theses X and XI of his "Theses on Feuerbach" make this emphatic:

X. The standpoint of the old materialism is "civil" society; the standpoint of the new is *human* society, or socialized humanity.

XI. The philosophers have only *interpreted* the world, in various ways; the point, however, is to *change* it.[11]

The goal of this change is the absolute freedom of man. In *The German Ideology,* Marx held that in post-revolutionary society, when man is finally beyond alienation, he will be able to be all things, a scholar, shepherd, critic, or whatever he chooses.[12] When this station is reached, man will have remade the world *and* himself. He will then be free to be whatever his reason chooses to be.

[10.] Karl Marx and F. Engels, *On Rebellion* (Moscow: Foreign Languages Publishing House, n.d.), 70.

[11.] *Ibid.,* 72.

[12.] See Gary North, *Marx's Religion of Revolution* (Nutley, NJ: The Craig Press, 1968), 60.

For Marx, the revolutionist must declare, "I am nothing but I must be everything."[13] Man must remake himself by destroying the past, the history which man as god did not create self-consciously. This means that there is nothing higher in man than man, nothing beyond man, and no law other than the will of man. The French Revolution must be carried to its logical conclusion. A new time must begin, signifying a new history and a new man. Man must be emancipated in order to become a man in this radical sense and in order to become free. As Marx declared:

> The only *practically* possible liberation of Germany is liberation from the point of view of the theory which proclaims man to be the highest essence of man. In Germany emancipation from the *Middle Ages* is possible only as emancipation from the *partial* victories over the Middle Ages as well. In Germany *no* kind of bondage can be shattered without *every* kind of bondage being shattered. The *fundamental* Germany cannot revolutionize without revolutionizing *from the foundation. The emancipation of the German* is *the emancipation of man.* The *head* of this emancipation is *philosophy,* its *heart* is the *proletariat.* Philosophy cannot be made a reality without the abolition of the proletariat, the proletariat cannot be abolished without philosophy being made a reality.
>
> When all inner requisites are fulfilled, the *day of German resurrection* will be proclaimed by the *crowing of the cock of Gaul.*[14]

In 1800, in *Fragments of a System,* Hegel had held that man's triumph would mean the triumph of the idea of infinite life united with men. "This self-elevation of man, not from the finite to the infinite (for these terms are only products of mere reflection, and as such their separation is absolute), but from finite life to infinite life, is religion."[15] Walt Whitman expressed this Hegelian principle thus: "I believe in you, my

---

13. From "Contribution to the *Critique of Hegel's Philosophy of the Right*", in Marx and Engels, *op. cit.*, 55.

14. *Ibid.*, 58.

15. G.W.F. Hegel, *On Christianity, Early Theological Writings* (New York: Harper Torchbooks, 1961), 311.

Soul."[16] In "Roaming in Thought (After Reading Hegel),"
Whitman wrote in 1881:

> Roaming in thought over the Universe, I saw the little
>   that is Good steadily hastening towards immortality,
> And the vast all that is call'd Evil I saw hastening to
>   merge itself and become lost and dead.[17]

Whitman also reflected the post-Kantian emphasis on
existential experience in "Of the Terrible Doubt of
Appearances" (1860). The epistemological question, Whitman
declared, is meaningless in the face of existential experience. As
long as he has male lovers, and his experiences with them,
questions of truth are meaningless in the face of the wisdom of
experience:

> — To me, these, and the like of these, are curiously
>   answer'd by my lovers, my dear friends;
> When he whom I love travels with me, or sits a long
>   while holding me by the hand,
> When the subtle air, the impalpable, the sense that
>   words and reason hold not, surround us and
>   pervade us,
> Then I am charged with untold and untellable wisdom—
>   I am silent—I require nothing further,
> I cannot answer the question of appearances, or that of
>   identity beyond the grave;
> But I walk or sit indifferent – I am satisfied,
> He ahold of my hand has completely satisfied me.[18]

Marx, after Kant and Hegel, wanted to remake the world in
terms of scientific socialism. Walt Whitman, in terms of Kant
and Hegel, wanted to remake it into a homosexual socialism.
Philosophy had now become a do-your-own-thing realm, with
every man his own god and universe.

John Dewey (1859-1952), in *The Public and its Problems*
(1927, 1930), spoke of Walt Whitman as "the seer" of
democracy. He held that both reason *and* man are

[16.] Walt Whitman, *Leaves of Grass*, "Walt Whitman," line 5 (New York:
Grosset & Dunlap, n.d.), 9.
[17.] *Ibid.*, 531.
[18.] *Ibid.*, 268f.

instrumental; the goal is the Great Community, the great god history realized in a united and socialistic mankind. Mankind, "the Public," according to Dewey, "will remain in eclipse," man will not truly be man, until the Great Community is realized. Until then, "the public will remain shadowy and formless."[19] As against the Biblical approach to man's problems, which consists of changing man through conversion, Dewey set forth "the method of changing the world through action" rather than "changing the self in emotion and idea."[20] There must be no law or standard external to or beyond man. Any other system than total democracy involves the subordination of the many to the few by coercion. In pure democracy, in the Great Community, coercion will apparently be absent.[21] This does not mean that each individual will simply do as he pleases, but rather, in true democracy, "the basic freedom is that of freedom of *mind* and of whatever degree of freedom of action and experience is necessary to produce freedom of intelligence."[22] Dewey thus has philosophical freedom in mind, and either *all* men become philosophers *a la* Dewey, or only a few like unto Dewey can be truly free. For Dewey, "[t]he foundation of democracy is faith in the capacities of human nature; faith in human intelligence and in the power of pooled and cooperative experience."[23] This is not a faith in man as such. It is a faith in philosophic man, man remade in the image of the modern philosopher. Nietzsche called him "superman" while modestly refraining from adding that he alone was superman in his day. Rousseau's incarnation of the will of the people in the philosopher-kings, in the general will or democratic consensus, is thus the only tolerable free man recognized by this tradition.

[19.] John Dewey, *The Public and Its Problems* (New York: Minton, Balch, 1930), 142.

[20.] Joseph Ratner, editor, *Intelligence in the Modern World, John Dewey's Philosophy* (New York: Modern Library, 1939), 275.

[21.] *Ibid.*, 401f.

[22.] *Ibid.*, 404.

[23.] *Ibid.*, 402.

God is denied, and infallibility is transferred to the historical process. For Marx, this infallible process finds its incarnation in the dictatorship of the proletariat; for Dewey, in the Great Community. The new god is a philosopher-king who rejects the idea of anything transcending himself. Nietzsche stated the matter more bluntly than others: "But that I may reveal my heart entirely unto you, my friends: *if* there were Gods, how could I endure it to be no God! *Therefore* there are no Gods."[24]

The problem was that there were now too many gods, every man becoming his own god as he "found" himself in terms of modern philosophy. How could mankind grow towards Dewey's Great Community, or Marx's communistic world, when no standard remained to judge growth and to distinguish it from decay? If only autonomous man is ultimate and real, and if meaning is replaced by methodology, how can we distinguish one idea from another, or have any means of describing anything in other than purely subjective terms? What is *good*, or what is *growth*, is then so only in my own mind. I cannot call it good for myself, because I have no means of making such a judgment: I can only say that I think of it as good for myself. The world has been reduced to my passing thoughts. The new world of modern philosophy has become a very small one indeed.

---

24. Friedrich Nietzsche, *Thus Spake Zarathustra*, in *The Philosophy of Nietzsche* (New York: Modern Library, n. d.), 98.

4

Existentialism:
The New God Creates
His Own Nature

The existentialist Albert Camus documented the contrast between the world of Christian faith and the world of modern man as tellingly perhaps as anyone has or could. The well-known opening words of *The Rebel, An Essay on Man in Revolt*, give us a sharp glance at the consequences of the new perspective:

> There are crimes of passion and crimes of logic. The boundary between them is not clearly defined. But the Penal Code made the convenient distinction of premeditation. We are living in the era of premeditation and the perfect crime. Our criminals are no longer helpless children who could plead love as their excuse. On the contrary, they are adults and they have a perfect alibi: philosophy, which can be used for any purpose—even for transforming murderers into judges.

> Heathcliff, in *Wuthering Heights*, would kill everybody on earth in order to possess Cathy, but it would never occur to him to say that murder is reasonable or theoretically defensible. He would commit it, and there his convictions end. This implies the power of love, and also strength of character. Since intense love is rare, murder remains an exception and preserves its aspect of infraction. But as

soon as a man, through lack of character, takes refuge in doctrine, as soon as crime reasons about itself, it multiplies like reason itself and assumes all the aspects of the syllogism. Once crime was as solitary as the cry of protest; now it is as universal as science. Yesterday it was put on trial; today it determines the law.[1]

As Camus pointed out, in the universe of Christianity, judgment is transcendental, and the final judgment is postponed; there is no necessity for an immediate reckoning. In the new universe of modern man, however, "the judgment pronounced by history must be pronounced immediately, for culpability coincides with the check to progress and with punishment."[2]

There are only two possible worlds, Camus held: the Christian world, the sacred realm, or the world of grace on the one hand; and, on the other, the world of rebellion or revolution. As one disappears, the other appears, and the waning of either means the rise of the other.[3] The credo of the world of rebellion, and its epistemology, is "I rebel—therefore we exist."[4] The world of modern man is unreasonable and absurd; it is a universe without meaning, one in which all is chaos. No valid knowledge is possible for modern man in terms of his philosophy. "The world itself, whose single meaning I do not understand, is but a vast irrational. If one could only say just once: 'This is clear,' all would be saved."[5] Man cannot know one fact in terms of the modern world-view. For him, "to think is first of all to create a world (or to limit one's own world, which comes to the same thing)."[6]

But the world of man in rebellion is not a free world:

---

[1] Albert Camus, *The Rebel, An Essay on Man in Revolt* (New York: Vintage Books, 1956), 3.
[2] *Ibid.*, 241.
[3] *Ibid.*, 21.
[4] *Ibid.*, 22.
[5] Albert Camus, *The Myth of Sisyphus* (New York: Alfred A. Knopf, 1958), 27.
[6] *Ibid.*, 99.

> If nothing is true, if the world is without order, then nothing is forbidden; to prohibit an action, there must, in fact, be a standard of values and an aim. But, at the same time, nothing is authorized; there must also be values and aims in order to choose another course of action. Absolute domination by the law does not represent liberty, but no more does absolute anarchy.[7]

Meaning is then gone, and freedom is as meaningless as good and evil. "At the point where it is no longer possible to say what is black and what is white, the light is extinguished and freedom becomes a voluntary prison."[8] The legitimacy of action is gone when we deny the ideas of good and evil; in abolishing illegitimacy, we also abolish legitimacy. Then "there is no choice, and that is where the bitterness comes in."[9] Ideas have their consequences, and a man pays a price for the ideas he holds: "a man is always a prey to his truths."[10] If he denies all truth, if he reduces the universe to chance, chaos, and the absurd, he is a prisoner of those ideas, and his life is limited by them. For the new man to become his own god thus has far-reaching consequences. It means the attempt to conquer and rule, and to create a heaven on earth, and to do so with every means possible, since everything is permitted. The goal is the unity of all creation, but goals have less and less meaning as the world of the Bible is abandoned. The rebellion of autonomous reason finds itself in a universe of unreason in which no single claim or hope of man's reason has any tenable meaning. Camus's wan hope in this situation is for man to declare that he is not god, and for all men to establish by agreement some limits or limiting concepts as restraints over themselves.[11] This answer, however, collapses, because the fact remains that the limits and the disclaimers are as meaningless as everything else in this new universe of modern man.

---

[7] Camus, *The Rebel*, 71.
[8] *Ibid.*
[9] Camus, *Myth of Sisyphus*, 67.
[10] *Ibid.*, 31.
[11] Camus, *The Rebel*, 306.

In Sartre, there is no desire to renounce man's claim to deity. Man is the being whose passion it is to become god.[12] Because the world is not God's creation, it has no meaning and no truth. There is no predestined or foreordained pattern in the universe, nor is there one in man. Man thus has *being* but no *essence*, no preestablished nature or purpose. It is man's privilege to make his own nature, to create his own essence. Man's freedom is his choice to become god.[13] "Man is the being whose project is to be God."[14] Man is the creator of his world, and thus "[t]he world is human."[15]

In man, existence precedes essence. In Sartre's words:

> What is meant here by saying that existence precedes essence? It means that, first of all, man exists, turns up, appears on the scene, and, only afterwards, defines himself. If man, as the existentialist conceives him, is indefinable, he himself will have made what he will be. Thus, there is no human nature, since there is no God to conceive it. Not only is man what he conceives himself to be, but he is also only what he wills himself to be after this thrust toward existence.
>
> Man is nothing else but what he makes of himself. Such is the first principle of existentialism.[16]

Moreover, "[e]xistentialism is nothing else than an attempt to draw all the consequences of a coherent atheistic position."[17]

If man at first is *nothing* in a world without reason or meaning, how can man, a nothing, project a reason and meaning even onto his own mind? To posit a universal unreason is to render man's attempt at reason absurd. How can man make himself into something with essence or meaning, when the very idea of essence has already been made untenable? Moreover, precisely because God and ultimate law

---

[12.] Jean-Paul Sartre, *Being and Nothingness* (New York: Philosophical Library, 1956), 566ff., 615, 625.
[13.] *Ibid.*, 599.
[14.] *Ibid.*, 566.
[15.] *Ibid.*, 218.
[16.] Jean-Paul Sartre, *Existentialism and Human Emotions* (New York: Philosophical Library, 1957), 15.
[17.] *Ibid.*, 51.

are denied, Sartre must insist that "all human activities are equivalent." As a result, he concludes, "[t]hus it amounts to the same thing whenever one gets drunk alone or is a leader of nations."[18]

Existence is totally without essence; it is totally fortuitous. Sartre is emphatic that there is not the least reason for our being here. Life is absurd; the ideas of law and necessity are vain and without reason. As a result, the essence a man creates for himself is entirely for himself, and it therefore makes no difference whether he becomes a solitary drunkard or a leader of nations.

Man is thus haunted by the fact of unreason, and also the fact of death. Both reduce man's being to nothingness and mock his being by their negation of it. As a result, man's quest for essence is doomed in advance, and Sartre must conclude, "[m]an is a useless passion," in all his being and especially as he attempts to become god.[19] Man has no meaning; all he has is an *absolute* freedom, but a freedom without purpose, direction, or rationality. Man is alone, because, despite all Sartre's attempts to build a bridge to other men and establish a tenable socialism, he must conclude that the neighbor is *the other*, the enemy, in fact, the devil.[20] The world becomes entirely the mind of man, and progress is not a social concept or an historical fact, but rather a personal feeling. According to Sartre, "[m]y grandfather believes in Progress; so do I: Progress, that long steep path which leads to me."[21]

Only subjective man remains, but how much of man? For Sartre, man's being is exhausted in his actions. In his own words,:

> The doctrine I am presenting is the very opposite of quietism, since it declares, "There is no reality except in action." Moreover, it goes further, since it adds, "Man is

---

18. Sartre, *Being and Nothingness*, 627.
19. *Ibid.*, 615.
20. See Kurt F. Reinhardt, *The Existentialist Revolt*, new enlarged edition (New York: Frederick Ungar, 1960), 167f.
21. Jean-Paul Sartre, *The Words* (Greenwich, CT: Fawcett, 1966), 21.

nothing else than his plan; he exists only to the extent that he fulfills himself; he is therefore nothing else than the ensemble of his acts, nothing else than his life."

Now, for the existentialist there is really no love other than one which manifests itself in a person's being in love. There is no genius other than one which is expressed in works of art; the genius of Proust is the sum of Proust's works; the genius of Racine is his series of tragedies. Outside of that, there is nothing. Why say that Racine could have written another tragedy, when he didn't write it? A man is involved in life, leaves his impress on it, and outside of that there is nothing.... However, when we say, "You are nothing else than your life," that does not imply that the artist will be judged solely on the basis of his works of art; a thousand other things will contribute toward summing him up. What we mean is that a man is nothing else than a series of undertakings, that he is the sum, the organization, the ensemble of the relationships which make up these undertakings.[22]

Since man has no essence, unless he creates it, man's being can only be known in "the ensemble of his acts," *i.e.*, in the plan or essence he reveals. What Sartre has said is that a man's being is his essence, and that without a manifested essence a man is nothing! Having taken great pains to deny that there is any predetermined pattern or essence in man created by God, Sartre now denies being to man unless such an essence is created. The plan or pattern returns in Sartre's world with a vengeance. It is not God's plan, but it is still a necessary plan. The idea of a necessary essence, having been abolished from the universe, is reintroduced as necessary to man's claim to be god.

In fact, according to Sartre, "the initial project of being God, which 'defines' man, comes close to being the same as a human 'nature' or an 'essence.'"[23] The freedom of man is his freedom to choose to be god. At the same time, "[t]he only being which can be called free is the being which nihilates its being. Moreover, we know that nihilation is lack of being and cannot

---

[22.] Sartre, *Existentialism and Human Emotions*, 31-33.
[23.] Sartre, *Being and Nothingness*, 566.

be otherwise. Freedom is precisely the being which makes itself a lack of being."[24] "Man makes himself. He isn't ready made at the start.... We define man in relationship to involvement."[25] However, for man to make himself means something very close to suicide!

We are, says the existentialist Wahl, "existence without essence."[26] The goal of man, his essence in effect, is to become god, but the goal of existentialist philosophy is "to destroy the ideas of Essence and Substance" and become a "philosophy of existence."[27]

Thus, man's being is defined by his essence, his goal of becoming god; he can only be known in relationship to his actions, to a pattern of development. The idea of a pattern or essence must, however, be negated, and man must also nihilate his being.

The new god has thus created his own nature in Sartre, a will to death. According to Levi,

> Sartre's philosophy is a cool demonstration that destructiveness is no accident but an ontological necessity and that all human experience is founded upon nothingness. Heidegger saw before Sartre our dread before the general threat of nothingness, but even he has not shown the nihilating activity of the human consciousness at the very center of the self.[28]

For Sartre, "[n]othingness is prior to being," and Levi sees in Sartre's philosophy "a veritable lust after nothingness. Perhaps it is even a sickness unto death."[29] With this, we do not disagree.

[24.] *Ibid.*, 567.

[25.] Sartre, *Existentialism and Human Emotion*, 43f.

[26.] Jean Wahl, *A Short History of Existentialism* (New York: Philosophical Library, 1949), 13.

[27.] *Ibid.*, 33f.

[28.] Albert William Levi, *Philosophy and the Modern World* (Bloomington, IN: University of Indiana Press, 1959), 410.

[29.] *Ibid.*, 423.

5

Sade to Genet:
The New Morality

Ideas do have consequences. Philosophy is not only an academic discipline but also the plan for living, and the most abstract ideas, within a few years of their acceptance by intellectuals and teachers, become the marching orders of civilization. The modern tendency of abstracting philosophy from life is therefore untenable.

One of the immediate consequences of modern philosophy was in the sphere of morality. In its earlier phase, Nature had replaced God as the basic and ultimate source of law and meaning. Deism retained God as a limiting concept, a formally necessary idea of logic rather than reality. The concept of causality from Descartes to Hume required a first cause, and God's function was thus limited to providing this logical necessity. Apart from serving as the first cause, God was irrelevant, and Nature provided all the functions which theology had ascribed to God. Natural law replaced God's law; natural law seen as inherent in Nature provided man and his world all the order and structure he needed.

Two things served to undermine the supremacy of Nature. *First*, the epistemology of modern thought led to the disappearance of Nature as such, as an overall unity and governing body of laws, in favor of fleeting sense impressions. The mind of autonomous man had come to replace Nature as the central principle and organizing entity. For Kant, the mind of man provided the structure, not Nature. Things-in-themselves are beyond knowability, so that any structure or law they may possess eludes us. It is our mind which is logical, not Nature, and it is thus our mind which provides the law and structure we "see" in Nature.

Second, with Darwin, Nature was reduced to chance variations, so that in a sense Nature was now known, as far as it could be known, to be purposeless and structureless. Man and society must thus be organized by the mind of man, not by a mythical concept of natural law. Thus, from a relatively free society in which Nature provided most of the government, civilization moved to an idea of society in which man, through the state, or anarchistic man alone, provided the government. The result was a shift from classical liberalism to socialism and/ or anarchism, in either case man being the source of law and structure.

Before this shift had fully transpired, however, the idea of Nature had been pushed to its limits and destroyed by the Marquis de Sade. The Marquis, Donatien Alphonse Françoise de Sade (1740-1814), readily saw the weakness in the deification of Nature. With God, an absolute and sovereign law prevails over the universe and judges all things therein. The normative is then beyond Nature, and Nature is the area of the defective, errant, or sinful, and it cannot claim ultimacy or perfection. However, once Nature is made ultimate, all things within Nature are made ultimate and normative, and no standard remains whereby Nature can be judged. Whatever is must thus be *right*, simply because *it is*. Alexander Pope (1688-1744), in his *An Essay on Man*, made this Deistic affirmation: "Whatever is, is right." More recently, Lenny Bruce held to the same faith: "Truth is 'what is.'"[1] The beatnik and hippie movements adhered to the same philosophy. Morality is ruled out of court:

[1.] Lenny Bruce, "How to Talk dirty and Influence People," *Playboy*, January 1964, 182.

all things are permitted, and there is no ground for objecting to anything.

Sade's hatred of God led him to eradicate every trace of Christian morality and law from the contemporary idea of Nature. His hatred of God's order in the universe was intense. One of his characters is made to exclaim, "Ah, how many times, by God, have I not longed to be able to assail the sun, snatch it out of the universe, make a general darkness, or use that star to burn the world! Oh, that would be a crime...."[2] Sade's writings are a long justification of evil and a defense of the right of evil to do what it will.

The groundwork had been laid for Sade by other men. Charles de Montesquieu (1689-1755), in *The Spirit of Laws*, had made laws dependent on climate, circumstance, and physiology. He discussed the relationship of law to soil, to nationality, to religion, to the size of a population, and much else, and thus prepared the way for a radical relativism which was not his intention. Sade, as a sadomasochist, a homosexual, a coprophiliac, and much more, was ready to use modern philosophy by forcing it to its logical conclusion: all acts are permitted.

But this is not all. When men cut themselves loose from Christian inhibitions and commit evil acts without restraint, then they are not only most natural, most in conformity with nature, but they are inspired. *This doctrine of natural inspiration* is basic to Sade. Evil is a natural mandate and inspiration: it is the infallible voice of Nature in us which Christianity falsely seeks to suppress. True philosophy will thus insist on the necessity and inspiration of evil. In Sade's *Philosophy in the Bedroom*, Dolmance instructs a girl in this new faith:

> DOLMANCE: Start from one fundamental point, Eugenie: in libertinage, nothing is frightful, because everything libertinage suggests is also a natural inspiration;

2. Simone de Beauvoir, "Must We Burn Sade?," in Austryn Wainhouse and Richard Seaver, translators and editors, *The Marquis de Sade, The 120 Days of Sodom and Other Writings* (New York: Grove Press, 1966), 32.

the most extraordinary, the most bizarre acts, those which most arrantly seem to conflict with every law, every human institution (as for Heaven, I have nothing to say), well, Eugenie, even those are not frightful, and there is not one amongst them all that cannot be demonstrated within the boundaries of Nature; it is certain that the one you allude to, lovely Eugenie, is the very same relative to which one finds such a strange fable in the tasteless fictions of the Holy Writ....

EUGENIE: Oh, 'tis natural?

DOLMANCE: Yes, natural, so I affirm it to be; Nature has not got two voices, you know, one of them condemning all day what the other commands....To convince ourselves, let us for an instant scrutinize both her operations and her laws. Were it that Nature did naught but create, and never destroy, I might be able to believe, with those tedious sophists, that the sublimest of all actions would be incessantly to labor at production, and following that, I should grant, with them, that the refusal to reproduce would be, would perforce have to be, a crime; however, does not the most fleeting glance at natural operations reveal that destructions are just as necessary to her plan as are creations? that the one and the other of these functions are interconnected and enmeshed so intimately that for either to operate without the other would be impossible? that nothing would be born, nothing would be regenerated without destructions? Destruction, hence, like creation, is one of Nature's mandates.[3]

Because Nature is normative, no crime exists except Christianity with its ideas of good and evil. Love is a myth; no religion, no law, and no state can exist. Men are "necessary creatures of Nature."[4] Their natures require fulfillment of their urge to evil. There can be no capital punishment, or any punishment, because murder is a natural act, as is slander. Theft cannot be forbidden. Every sexual perversion is a

---

[3.] Richard Seaver and Austryn Wainhouse, translators and editors, *The Marquis de Sade, the Complete Justine, Philosophy in the Bedroom, and Other Writings* (New York: Grove Press, 1965), 273-275.

[4.] *Ibid.*, 308.

delight, not a crime, and it is a crime to resist Nature. "We listen only to Nature's voice, we are fully convinced that if anything were criminal, it would be to resist the penchants she inspires in us, rather than to come to grips with them."[5] Natural inspiration requires us to commit every evil act we feel an urge to do. (Sade cites Thomas More's *Utopia* for justification).[6] Incest and sodomy are justified, and one of the virtues of incest for Sade is that "it loosens family ties."[7] Bestiality is also justified, and, after Montesquieu, man's nature is seen in terms of physiology: "The penchant for sodomy is the result of physical formation, to which we contribute nothing and which we cannot alter."[8] Infanticide, abortion, euthanasia, and statist schools are all approved by Sade. Overpopulation is remedied by his sexual program, he declared. Man's evil imagination is for Sade man's total world.

But life is not good for Sade. He saw nature and life as in essence frustration, a point made in *Eugenie de Franval* (1788) and all his works. There is not only a will to evil but also a will to universal death, to blot out the sun, to kill all men sadistically, and to perish in the universal destruction.

The universe of modern man has become not only small, as small as his own mind, but also totally perverse, with a radical will to evil and a will to death.

The impact of Sade on the twentieth century is very great. The "underground" press, the sexually oriented magazines for men and women, television, films, and literature all manifest Sadean characteristics. To cite an example, Martin Shephard, M.D., addresses "The Incest Urge" in *Gallery*. Homosexual, lesbian, and sadomasochistic groups now have national organizations, and Shephard hopes that incest will soon gain a like "respectability." In citing one case of father-daughter incest, Shephard writes, "[o]ne wonders where the greater abnormality exists—among the incestuous couple or within

---

5. *Ibid.*, 316
6. *Ibid.*, 323.
7. *Ibid.*, 324.
8. *Ibid.*, 326.

the society that so harshly condemned their relationship with each other."[9] He looks forward to the day when incest is so routine and normal that someone will casually say, "I used to screw Mommy, and now we're still good friends."[10]

In science, the Sadean principle is equally present. The Kinsey Report advocated premarital sexual freedom for young girls and stated that child-molestation was not a crime. The crime, it held, was society's disapproval of such acts, which warped a little girl's mind against the experience.[11]

The shape of modern thought, as it envisions its future, appears clearly in Sartre's study of Jean Genet, a homosexual and a criminal. Genet, in prison, came to the conclusion that, if modern thought is right, then there is no crime, and, instead of being an evil man and a convict, he was the man of the future. His writings gained him a wide audience and freedom. For Sartre, Genet is a saint in the new and modern order. "When Evil was possible in his eyes, Genet did Evil in order to be wicked. Now that Evil proves impossible, Genet will do Evil in order to be a saint."[12] As a criminal, Genet practiced evil to offend God and man. As a saint, Genet now recognizes that there is no crime, and he performs the same acts to free men from the illusion of evil, as the saint who leads mankind into a new life. Evil is now impossible because there is no God, and thus no law to violate. Genet as a criminal stole to defy all order. "I went to theft as to a liberation."[13] His first liberation was from God; his second liberation was from the idea that the evil he did was truly evil at all.

---

[9] Martin Shephard, M.D., "The Incest Urge," *Gallery*, 2, no. 6 (June 1974): 114.

[10] *Ibid.*, 118.

[11] Alfred C. Kinsey, Wardell B. Pomeroy, Clyde E. Martin, Paul Gebhard, etc., *Sexual Behavior in the Human Female* (Philadelphia, PA: W.B. Saunders, 1953), 115, 121, 327f, 330.

[12] Jean-Paul Sartre, *Saint Genet, Actor and Martyr* (New York: Mentor, 1964), 214.

[13] *Ibid.*, 435.

Genet, we are told, "has *killed the law*."[14] Moreover, "[t]he God of Genet is Genet himself."[15] "The pure will to evil," Sartre tells us, "represents spirituality."[16] Modern man must purify himself by systematically committing evil; only then can he be a saint in the modern sense.

Since man has denied God, why must he also deny the good? Why must he affirm evil as his principle and as his way of life? The answer, says Sartre, is that evil alone gives man autonomy. To pursue the good is to surrender one's independence from God and man. "Unless one is a god, one cannot make oneself happy without the help of the universe; to make oneself unhappy, one needs only oneself."[17] Modern man's chosen course is thus a deliberate unhappiness, a self-willed alienation and self-pity, an affirmation of evil with passion and intensity, and a suicidal course as the climax to unhappiness.

The world of Sartre is now "the strut world" of our cities. The "underground" press is an echo of Sade. Thus, one writer to the *L.A. Star*, 10 June 1974, finds "sexual activity tame without the added spice of urgency or danger." Homosexuality, bestiality, and like acts are praised in other papers as means of liberation. Narcotics are suggested for the same reason. The deliberately destructive, socially, personally, and physically, is in vogue and is intently pursued.

The effects of modern philosophy are now apparent in the streets, in the grade schools, and in every area of life. Philosophy is not only an academic question: it is a matter of life and death.

---

14. *Ibid.*, 146.
15. *Ibid.*, 161.
16. *Ibid.*, 168.
17. *Ibid.*, 175.

6

From Artisan to Artist:
Art in the Modern Culture

Men often think of the past in terms of the present, and they fail to see important inner changes because they judge things externally. The Christian centuries are often seen as an ideal era for *artists*, in that the medieval church was a constant source of work because the arts had a vital place in the life of the church and a centrality in the life of man which is now lacking. The fallacy in this perspective is that *the idea of the artist* is a modern one, a product of the Renaissance. Previously, not artists but *artisans* existed. The architects, sculptors, painters, and musicians were workmen and businessmen, often organized into unions or guilds, and marked by a practical and business-like approach to their craft. The modern idea of the artist was alien to them.

The transition from artisan to artist represented a major shift in cultural attitudes. The shift, *first* of all, was religious. For Christian civilization, inspiration was an attribute of the Bible: it was a God-breathed book and set forth God's truth for man and society. Man's thinking had to follow the pattern of God's word and work, and was an attempt to think God's thoughts after Him. With the rise of humanism, the authority of Scripture eroded, and with it the authority of church, priest, and, later, pastor. Humanism sought its own authentic voice, its own sources of inspiration, and one of the first claimants to be that voice was *the artist*. The artist was now less and less a businessman and artisan, and more and more a religious figure, a humanistic leader.

Second, the artist now presented himself increasingly as a new prophet. In the Romantics, such as Shelley, this temper was especially pronounced. In Shelley, a militant atheism was combined with a strong sense of *natural inspiration*, of prophetic destiny. Poets began openly to write as inspired men. For example, Shelley began *The Mask of Anarchy* thus:

> As I lay asleep in Italy
> There came a voice from over the Sea,
> And with great power it forth led me
> To walk in the visions of Poesy.

We miss the point of much poetry, and especially of the Romantics, if we take such statements as mere stage setting and poetic license. It was meant as seriously as St. John's declaration in the first verse of *Revelation*: "The Revelation of Jesus Christ, which God gave unto him, to shew unto his servants things which must shortly come to pass; and he sent and signified it by his angel unto his servant John." This is supernatural inspiration; the modern artists, like Shelley, claimed *natural inspiration*. The future of humanism required the development of natural inspiration, and the artist gave his life to its development.

Third, the artist as the voice of natural inspiration was thus increasingly at odds with conventional middle class Christian life. Such living was the epitome of the Christian past that the artist sought to supplant and destroy. As a result, *Bohemianism* became mandatory for more and more artists. It was necessary to create, foster, and aggravate a breach between art and orderly society. To illustrate, a moderately talented modern artist, who died prematurely, had a bewildered but loving family which was ready to tolerate his insults and continue to subsidize his life as an artist. Their very willingness to be helpful only aggravated him into more outrageous insults and offenses against them. He felt it necessary to provoke their hostility in order to feel free from them and open to natural inspiration. The artist thus began to wage warfare against orderly society in the name of natural inspiration and to live a life of studied immoralism as a matter of principle and artistic integrity.

Fourth, discipline in art was progressively dropped in favor of spontaneity, and the studied quality of early humanistic art gave way to totally mindless, meaningless art as most expressive of natural inspiration. A poem, people were told, should not mean, it should *be*, and the same was said to be true of all works of art. *Form*, as a result, was progressively despised and neglected. The careful attention to the craft of painting or writing gave way to a deliberate expression of *contempt* for craft. Natural inspiration was held to be so powerful a force that it could brook no restraint of form or craft.

Fifth, whereas humanism, as it developed out of medieval Scholasticism, was intensely rationalistic and saw the mind as evidence of man's supremacy, the new humanism looked to man's feelings and loins for man's power. The older tradition of rationalistic humanism came in for savage criticism by the new humanists. An illustration of this change can be found in the work of William Bouquereau (1825-1905) and criticisms thereof. When the offensiveness of Bouquereau is sufficiently in the distance, he may undergo a revival of interest, but, for the present, he is a type of the hated art of the Academy, the old-line humanism. His offense is clear-cut in his painting, *Nymphs and Satyr*.[1] Technically, the painting shows great skill, care, and execution, and a fine sense of balance. Its *idea* is a fitting symbol of rationalistic humanism. A strong, dark, muscular satyr is being pulled, controlled, and played with like a pet poodle by four nude girls, whose innocence alone prevents them from looking voluptuous. One of the girls is calling to other nude girls in the background, to show off the

---

[1.] See plate 20 in R.H. Ives Gommell, *Twilight of Painting* (New York: G.P. Putnam's Sons, 1946).

harmless prize they have in hand. The picture is a symbol of the powerlessness and harmlessness of violent and sinful emotions, forces, and lusts in the hands of innocence and reason. The light drags the dark one out into the open and renders him innocuous. A modern artist of the latter part of the twentieth century, if he were to be at all pictorial, would show the satyr in power and triumphant over the naked girls; power for him would reside in raw, brute emotion and force, not in reason; in Freud's *id* or pleasure principle, not in the *superego*, the conscious rational discipline of the community of men. In terms of humanistic principles, the twentieth century artist is more accurate than Bouquereau.

Sixth, the tendency of humanism to move downward from reason to the primitive emotions has led to the strong emphasis on primitivism in art. Primitivism is equated with vitality. The mindless Nature of the post-Darwinian world is anti-rational. Mind is a late-comer in the universe, and "animal instincts" have thus deeper roots and greater vitality. Thus, Eugene Delacroix, who saw the future more clearly than Bouquereau and was thus the more influential and effective artist, wrote in his *Journal* on 1 May 1850:

> It is evident that nature cares very little whether man has a mind or not. The real man is the savage; he is in accord with nature as she is. As soon as man sharpens his intelligence, increases his ideas and the way of expressing them, and acquires needs, nature runs counter to him in everything. He has to do violence to her continually.[2]

This statement, coming almost a decade before Darwin's theory was published, was not unusual in that day, and it explains why Darwin was so readily believed. He was giving voice to the myths of his age. If "the real man is the savage," then the goal of the artist is to become a primitive, a new savage, with all the intensity he can muster.

About three quarters of a century later, Guillaume Apollinaire declared, in *The Cubist Painters*, "[t]he time has

---

[2] John Gassner and Sidney Thomas, editors, *The Nature of Art* (New York: Crown Publishers, 1964), 433.

come for us to be the masters. And good will is not enough to make victory certain."[3] The artist, he held, must be like God: he must create in his own image. In doing this, he cannot follow the older ideal of rationalistic humanism but rather the new, post-Sadean ideal. "Artists are, above all, men who want to become inhuman."[4] The American, Homer Saint-Gaudens, declared, "[w]hat garlic is to salad, insanity is to art."[5]

Rationalism and reason had to be abandoned. *Purpose* in art must be rejected together with the idea of God. A God-ward direction is upward; primitivism requires a downward direction.

This means, *seventh*, an emphasis on the perverse and the abnormal. For Sartre, evil represents the area where man can express his autonomy and creativity, and the modern artist has agreed. According to author Eric Newton, the Romantics established this new interest: they "can never rejoice in the normal."[6] This taste for the abnormal goes hand in hand with an intense dislike for "whatever is law-abiding, whatever conforms to a pattern." Such an artist "refuses to acknowledge the existence of law as applied to self-expression." For him the only law is "Thou shalt be exceptional and follow that which is exceptional." The individual must have full freedom of self-expression in every area of the primitive and abnormal."[7] It is always that which is evil that appeals to the artist, not that which is good, because it is for him the area of freedom from God.

Eighth, while modern art has been close to the revolutionary impulses of the modern era, there has been a difference. Newton points this out: "the factor common to most romantic art is a rebellion against law, but what distinguishes the romantic pursuit of the abnormal is a desire to escape rather than to rebel."[8] His basic drive is hostility and destruction, *a*

[3.] *Ibid.*, 558.

[4.] *Ibid.*, 560.

[5.] *Ibid.*, 589.

[6.] Eric Newton, *The Romantic Rebellion* (New York: St. Martin's Press, 1962), 59.

[7.] *Ibid.*, 64.

[8.] *Ibid.*, 125.

desire to spit and run, and this impulse is being communicated by more and more artists to revolutionists. The artist, however, does not like to reveal his basic escapism, and he carefully conceals it behind a façade of rejection of society.

Ninth, natural inspiration seeks a perpetually new word, not an old word. If Pop Art becomes accepted, it must be rejected as an old law. Art must thus have a continually fresh natural inspiration, and this means new shock, fresh sensation, and an ever more brazen expression of anti-reason. A pattern, form, or style, once established, constitutes a form of bondage to be rejected vehemently. Modern art thus constitutes warfare against the past and present in the name of a mindless flight from God, reason, and order.

These tendencies of modern art reflect the tendencies of modern culture. Although present in exaggerated and theatrical fashion in the artist, they are present everywhere in society. Humanism is at war with all its yesterdays and todays. The humanistic students of the modern university wage war against their humanistic professors.

The Triton College (Illinois) student publication, *Kaleidoscope Komix* (Special Student Issue, 1973) expresses this mood. The cover shows an angry student chained on a large copy of Webster's *Dictionary.* Over him stand his torturers, four professors in academic garb. The point of the cover and the content is that *any* discipline or pattern in education represents the dead hand of the past. Instead of classroom teaching and the older humanistic credos, the students demand freedom for community action. The irony of this pseudo-rebellion, and the depiction of the student being sacrificed to standards, is that the students already have what they want! Triton College has a Kaleidoscope Department offering two semesters of work in terms of the community action idea. The cover of the comic book, however, shows a student as the human sacrifice. Is it not rather education which has been sacrificed? And is not the modern humanistic movement in reality the sacrifice of man to a mythical animal past?

In February, 1849, Herman Melville, a representative of the modern mood in art, wrote Evert Duykinck that "if another Messiah ever comes 'twill be in Shakespeare's person."[9] Melville, who wrote intensely symbolic books of ostensibly typical prophecy, believed that humanistic revelation would come by natural inspiration. The delving into the underworld of man's imagination which he himself pursued has brought forth, however, not a new Shakespeare as the messiah of humanism, but a rise of occultism and Satanism. Melville's purpose, according to Baird, was to make "new symbols to replace the 'lost' symbols of Protestant Christianity."[10] The symbols he created were all subterranean and hinted of a deeper darkness. The darkness has since come, and W.B. Yeats has seen it as the second coming of the beast, slouching towards the new Bethlehem, waiting to be born.

[9.] Leon Howard, *Herman Melville* (Minneapolis, MN: University of Minnesota Press, 1961), 22.

[10.] James Baird, *Ishmael, A Study of the Symbolic Mode in Primitivism* (New York: Harper Torchbooks, 1960), xv.

7

The Impact of Philosophy on Religion:
The Principle of Modernity

With the rise of modern philosophy, a reversal of roles took place between theology and philosophy. In a few medieval thinkers such as Anselm, and in much Calvinistic thought, theology determined philosophy. Earlier, in Scholasticism, philosophy had gained the upper hand as a result of Aristotle's influence. With the Enlightenment, modern philosophy began its capture of church life and theology, which, as a result, became an echo chamber of culture, reflecting rationalism, experientialism, the new inspiration, and the charisma of the new.

The starting point of modern philosophy with Descartes was the autonomous mind of man as ultimate and as judge and arbiter over reality. It was this autonomous reason which became the starting point for theology as well. The foundations for this rationalistic approach were fully developed by Bishop Joseph Butler (1692-1752) in *The Analogy of Religion*. Butler presupposed, *first*, the autonomous mind of man as the judge, competent to decide whether or not God exists and religion is true; and *second*, he assumed that this autonomous reason is or can be neutral and unprejudiced. With these presuppositions he could conclude, "to an unprejudiced mind, ten thousand thousand instances of design cannot but prove a designer."[1]

Third, the certainty of this autonomous reason is its own existence and ultimacy. All other knowledge has, at its best, only *probability*. Butler's "Introduction" made this point as a preliminary to the "evidence" for natural religion and Christianity:

> Probable evidence is essentially distinguished from demonstrative by this, that it admits of degrees; and of all variety of them, from the highest moral certainty, to the very lowest presumption. We cannot indeed say a thing is probably true upon one very slight presumption for it; because, as there may be probabilities on both sides of a question, there may be some against it; and though there be not, yet a slight presumption does not beget that degree of conviction which is implied in saying a thing is probably true. But that the slightest possible presumption is of the nature of a probability, appears from hence; that such law presumption often repeated, will amount even to a moral certainty. Thus a man's having observed the ebb and flow of the tide to-day, affords some sort of presumption, though the lowest imaginable, that it may happen again tomorrow; but the observation of this event for so many days, and months, and ages together, as it has been observed by mankind, gives a full assurance that it will.
>
> That which chiefly constitutes Probability is expressed in the word Likely, *i.e.*, like some truth, or true event (*verisimile*); like it, in itself, in its evidence, in some more or fewer of its circumstances. For when we determine a thing to be probably true, suppose that an event has or will come to pass, it is from the mind's remarking in it a likeness to some other event, which we have observed has come to pass. And this observation forms, in numberless daily instances, a presumption, opinion, or full conviction, that such event has sometimes, most commonly, or always, so far as our observation reaches,

---

[1] Joseph Butler, *The Analogy of Religion* (London: George Bell & Sons, 1897), 320.

come to pass at like distances of time, or place, or upon like occasions.[2]

The world of the mind is the world of certainty and the known; the world of God is the world of probability at best, and the unknown. Butler's starting point is the mind of man; from man he reasons to Nature, and then from Nature to God. All this makes the probabilities with respect to God to rest on the probabilities with respect to Nature. Butler makes note of Descartes's method,[3] while dissenting from it to a degree in order to follow John Locke.

Fourth, Butler not only reasons from the known to the unknown, but he assumes, as Van Til has shown, "that the unknown will be to a considerable extent unlike the known," because it transcends it, but its basic constitution is similar to that which we know, so that, with respect to Christianity, "we are, according to Butler, in a position to believe it primarily because it is *like* the constitution and course of nature."[4] This is anthropomorphic religion: God is made in man's image, rather than *vice versa*, and the conclusion of the new theology has indeed been the exaltation of the future man and his society as god.

However, just as the objective world began to crumble in philosophy, so, too, in the realm of theology, it came to have less and less significance in the face of the overwhelming and autonomous inner reality. The result was Pietism, the religion of the heart, of feeling, of *experimental* or *experiential religion*. To know the truth now came to mean *experience*. Truth as experience had an erosive effect on the historical nature of Christianity. In Friedrich Ernst Daniel Schleiermacher (1769-1834), the strands of Pietism and Kantianism merge to war against metaphysics and dogma in religion. Schleiermacher set up a "religious phenomenalism. It is no virtue to decree the autonomous intellect if one sets up in its stead an autonomous

2. *Ibid.*, 72.
3. *Ibid.*, 75.
4. Cornelius Van Til, *Christian-Theistic Evidences* (Philadelphia, PA: Westminster Theological Seminary, 1947), 4.

feeling. And that is precisely what Schleiermacher does. In his theology it is still the human personality as such that has the final criterion or truth within itself."[5]

For Schleiermacher, the natural inspiration of the heart and its communion with the Absolute outweighed all dogmas. He ignored the doctrine of the inspiration of Scripture in favor of his implicit doctrine of the natural inspiration of the religious sentiments of man. Some have attempted to hold that Schleiermacher had a God-centered theology because his idea of the religious consciousness of man is that it is a *feeling of absolute dependence*. But Schleiermacher does not say that it actually is *absolute dependence*, but rather that it is a *feeling* of absolute dependence. He separated religion from metaphysics and from any need or necessity to have true knowledge of God in Himself and instead located religion entirely in the realm of feeling. The way was prepared for an existentialist faith. Doctrine was reduced to experience and consciousness. "Thus sin is understood rather as unholiness than as guilt before God; redemption rather as sanctification than as justification; Christ's death as a simple incident in his life of self-sacrifice; atonement as the setting-forth of the union of God with man; the mode of attaining to salvation as a spiritual realization of this union through the embracing of Christ in love. The Holy Ghost is presented as simply the collective Spirit of the Church, as resulting from the union of human nature with the divine."[6]

The stage was thus set for the assertion of the full principle of modernity. The Unitarians who went on to formulate the Religion of Humanity made this their first principle. O. B. Frothingham (1822-1895) wrote:

> The interior spirit of any age is the spirit of God; and no faith can be living that has that spirit against it; no Church

---

5. Cornelius Van Til, *The Defense of the Faith* (Philadelphia, PA: Presbyterian & Reformed Publishing Co., 1955), 146. See 139 in the revised and abridged edition of 1967.

6. J. P. Lacroix, "Schleiermacher," in John M'Clintock and James Strong, editors, *Cyclopaedia of Biblical, Theological, and Ecclesiastical Literature*, vol. IX (New York: Harper & Brothers, 1894), 414.

can be strong except in that alliance. The life of the time appoints the creed of the time and modifies the establishment of the time.[7]

Sade asserted the doctrine of natural inspiration for the individual. Whatever any individual, uninfluenced by Christianity, chooses to do is a product of natural inspiration and is not to be denied. Frothingham's doctrine of natural inspiration and infallibility is not individualistic but collectivist. It is the spirit of the age which is the Spirit of God, the general will which represents the truth of the age. In terms of this, Frothingham would logically have opposed Sade's sexual ideas when held by Sade alone, but, in a Sadean sexual revolution such as is now under way, he would logically have seen them as the spirit of God and the necessary creed for the church.

For Frothingham, truth is entirely relative to the historical movement of the day. History is the new god, and man as the historical animal is, in his general will, the expression of God.

In Paul Tillich, theology as anthropology moved a step forward. Karl Barth had still used the terminology of orthodoxy while speaking the language of a post-Kantian dialecticism. His God was thus a limiting concept, not a reality. In Tillich, *being* was denied to God, who was presented as neither being nor non-being.

The Death of God school openly declared that God is dead, dead because man has by definition excluded Him. According to Altizer, as he defines history,

> This meaning of 'historical' is intimately related to the modern idea of 'historicity'; for, in this perspective, 'historicity' means a total immersion in historical time, an immersion that is totally isolated from any meaning or reality that might lie beyond it.[8]

---

7. Octavius Brooks Frothingham, *The Religion of Humanity*, third edition (New York: G.P. Putnam's Sons, 1875), 7f.
8. Thomas J. J. Altizer, *Mircea Eliade and the Dialectic of the Sacred* (Philadelphia, PA: Westminster Press, 1963), 23.

In terms of this, only man can be historical, and God is by definition non-historical. The idea of *the sacred* is separated from God and attached to time, so that history rather than God becomes the subject of religion. However, because the idea of the sacred is detached from God, it becomes profane, and the idea of the profane becomes the basis of much more theology.

In the new anthropology, man, as Feuerbach hoped, has taken the place of God, and the significance once attached to God is now assigned to man. Moreover, according to theologian Sam Keen,

> Modern man understands himself as belonging totally to the flux of history. Since he can believe only in what he can experience and think, and since his modes of thought are empirical, pragmatic and operational, he finds himself increasingly cut off from the possibility relating in hope to any transcendent reality. The ancient, amphibious character of man is denied. Modern man lives a profane life…the virtues of faith and hope are impossible for him.
>
> It would not be too extravagant to say that the fundamental thesis of the new view of man which is coming to dominate the 20th century intellectual is that modern man has become posthuman….[9]

God cannot be "conceived as being," according to Catholic theologian Leslie Dewart.[10] What then is the religious hope, if it is not God? The answers are many, and they are essentially similar, whether from Teilhard de Chardin or from American theologians. In the words of Father Metz, a University of Munster theologian, the hope of the church "must be realized in a creative-militant eschatology."[11] The University of Tübingen theologian Moltmann calls this neo-Marxist religious goal the *Theology of Hope*. The God of such a theology

---

9. Sam Keen, "Hope in a Posthuman Era," in Martin E. Marty and Dean G. Peerman, editors, *New Theology No. 5* (New York: Macmillan, 1968), 82.

10. Leslie Dewart, "God and the Supernatural," in *ibid.*, 155.

11. Johannes B. Metz, "Creative Hope," in *ibid.*, 137.

is *the future*, the realized future of man. He is a God who cannot be in us or over us "but always only before us."[12]

For Moltmann, neither the God of Scripture nor faith are basic. Rather, it is *hope*, man's hope of a better world order. Moreover, while this is an historical hope, Moltmann dissolves history into the experience of autonomous man. Bahnsen has called attention to the confusion that results:

> As the evangelical comes upon Moltmann's initial judgment about the resurrection of Christ he might gain some encouragement; Moltmann says, "Christianity stands or falls with the reality of the raising of Jesus from the dead by God. In the New Testament there is no faith that does not start *a priori* with the resurrection of Jesus." But no sooner does he make such a bold assertion than he begins to weaken the thought until all evangelical interest in the resurrection has been washed away. Moltmann goes on to say: "The question 'what can I know of the historical facts?' cannot be here separated from the ethical and existential question: 'what am I to do?' and from the eschatological question: 'what may I hope for?'...The question is then no longer whether this proclamation (of the resurrection) is correct in the 'historical' sense, but whether and how the proclamation is legitimized and necessarily called to life by the event of which it speaks.... The event of the raising of Christ from the dead is an event which is understood only in the modus of promise. Hence the reports of the resurrection will always have to be read also eschatologically in the light of the question, 'what may I hope for?'" A person is left confused and wondering whether among Moltmann's verbiage about "the association of the crucified one with the 'risen' one" he truly believes in the historical bodily resurrection or just what. One almost gets the impression that resurrection for Moltmann is synonymous with socio-political involvement rather than depicting an event.[13]

[12.] Jurgen Moltmann, *Theology of Hope* (New York: Harper and Row, 1967), 16.
[13.] Greg L. Bahnsen, "Moltmann's Hope of Theology," unpublished paper, 1969.

Leslie Dewart, in *The Future of Belief,* suggested dropping all use of the name of God, as well as picture images and word images of Him. For Dewart, "the name of *God* is possibly not a particularly meaningful one" for modern man.[14] God does not have being; He "is not charitable; he *is* charity."[15]

Another Catholic theologian has written, "[i]n *Man Becoming* I try to translate every sentence about God, contained in the traditional creeds, into a sentence dealing with human possibilities promised to man and changes of consciousness offered to him."[16] Baum, in describing his thinking, and the thought of Eugene Fontinell, Leslie Dewart, and Eulalio Baltazar, all Catholic theologians, finds all four in essential agreement that,

> What is wrong, for today, in the traditional manner, is the objectification of God. Because of the change in the understanding of man and his world, it has become impossible to think of God as a being over against and above human history. God is not objective: God cannot become an object of man's mind, of which he can acquire some knowledge, however analogous, and about which he is able to make true statements. God is not a supreme being, of which man can seek any kind of spectator knowledge.
>
> The four authors give various reasons why it has become impossible to think of God as the supreme being. The theoretical reasons are connected with the developmental or evolutionary view of reality, characteristic of the present. Other reasons are drawn from Christian piety itself. For a great number of Christians, traditional prayer has become almost impossible; they can no longer project God before them as the invisible friend or father and then address him in their prayers.[17]

---

14. Leslie Dewart, *The Future of Belief* (St. Louis, MO: Herder and Herder, 1968), 213.
15. *Ibid.,* 206.
16. Gregory Baum, "Toward a New Catholic Theism," *The Ecumenist, A Journal for Promoting Christian Unity* 8, no. 4 (May-June 1970): 55.
17. *Ibid.,* 55f.

Man is in the process of becoming: "Man is always more than man. There is a divine mystery operative in the becoming of man and his world."[18] "The doctrine of God is the Good News that humanity is possible."[19] While God does not have being, Baum declares that

> For Dewart, Baltazar and Baum God is personal; by this they mean that man's relationship to the deepest dimension of his history, the ever new and gratuitous summons present in his life, is personal, i.e., consists of listening and responding, of receiving gifts and being grateful for them, of being called, and, like Abraham, leaving the past and moving with confidence into the future.[20]

When God spoke to the young Samuel, Samuel answered, "Speak; for thy servant heareth" (1 Samuel 3:10). In terms of Baum's comment, the modern theologian apparently listens to his consciousness, hears the mystical voice of his self-created future, and, perhaps, contemplates his navel also, and then answers to himself, Speak, Lord, for thy servant heareth. This perhaps accounts for the fact that fewer and fewer men are ready to listen to the theologian: they are too busy listening to themselves.

---

18. *Ibid.*, 58.
19. *Ibid.*, 59.
20. *Ibid.*, 61. Catholic theologians are now trying to surpass Protestant theologians in blasphemy!

8

The Implications of Modern
Philosophy: The Will to Fiction

The will to fiction is a major aspect and motive of the
modern mind.[1]

Ostensibly, the direction of modern philosophy has been
hostile to the mind-body of Greek philosophy. In reality, it has
aggravated that problem. Because of its dialectical nature,
modern philosophy is tied irrevocably to the implicit dualism
of nature versus freedom, a dialectical tension which is the heir
of the Greek dialectic. *Mind* has become *freedom* in the modern
dialectic, and *body* or *matter* has become *nature*.

Moreover, because modern epistemology has reduced the
world of nature to the area of the probable, and made the area
of the mind the realm of the certain, it has warped the dialectic
without removing it. The mind as the area of certainty can
thus deal cavalierly with the world of the probable.

A practical and telling example of this is David Henry
Thoreau, or, as he later called himself, Henry David Thoreau

[1.] See R. J. Rushdoony, *The Word of Flux*, ch. 11, "The Fight From Reality," (Fairfax, VA: Thoburn Press, 1975); and R.J. Rushdoony, *The Politics
of Pornography*, ch. 9, "Life as Fiction" (New Rochelle, NY: Arlington
House, 1974). The discussions in these chapters are different, and the
present one supplements rather than repeats them.

(1817-1862). Thoreau was deeply influenced by Hegelian philosophies, but he is best known, not as a thinker, but for his work on *Walden, or Life in the Woods* (1854), a work very influential among twentieth century youth with a like will to fiction. Edel has observed of *Walden*, "*Walden* is not a document, nor even the record of a calculated experiment. It is a work of art pretending to be a documentary. Thoreau talked as if he lived in the wilderness but he lived in the suburbs. He furnished his home with pieces retrieved from Concord attics."[2] A romantic and an idler, his stay at Walden was local comedy. The would-be hermit walked to the grocery store almost daily to gossip and talk with other town idlers around the stove. He went home to his mother daily, and dined in the homes of friends. According to Edel,

> Literary criticism, if it wished to treat *Walden* (1854) as a work of the imagination, might say that every poet lives in fancy rather than in fact. But literary history, unlike literary criticism, is in bondage to truth, and the truth is that Thoreau lived one kind of life and transformed it in his work into another—and then scolded his fellows for not following his ideas. Like his mother, who often put on grand airs in the town, Chanticleer crowed out of a world of make-believe.[3]

Edel, not a hostile critic, points out, "[t]here are distinct pathological traits in Thoreau, a constant sense—a few have discerned it—of inner disintegration...."[4] This should not surprise us. In Thoreau, the mind's certainties are fictions, and they begin to mold the natural world's probabilities into their own image.

In Walt Whitman we have a like will to fiction. Walt Whitman (1819-1892) worked first in a lawyer's and then in a doctor's office, then for a painter. Subsequently, he became an itinerant country school teacher. In 1846 he became editor of the *Brooklyn Eagle*. His background was thus clerical and

---

[2] Leon Edel, *Henry D. Thoreau* (Minneapolis, MN: University of Minnesota Press, 1970), 29.
[3] *Ibid.*, 23.
[4] *Ibid.*, 43.

bookish to a greater degree than that of most Americans in his day. One writer whom he was especially partial to was the Romantic novelist, George Sand. From a George Sand character, a primitive poet who in trance spouts rhapsodic poetry, Whitman borrowed the idea of the true and Christ-poet of the new age, of humanism, as the inspired child of nature. He began to write in that vein, and to play that role, and the result was *Leaves of Grass* (1855).[5] Whitman's verbose and affected nonsense was accepted then and now because it accorded with the general will to fiction. When Shephard's study of Whitman's pose appeared, I was then a student in the English Department of the University of California. I asked a few professors about the book and loaned it to one: they all brushed it aside as irrelevant!

D. H. Lawrence (David Herbert Lawrence, 1885-1930) also illustrates the will to fiction. A man of marked personal incompetence, like Whitman he saw himself as a Christ-figure. In 1923, on leaving for New Mexico, Lawrence gave a Last Supper at the Café Royal for his disciples. He told them, "I am not a man.... I am Man." He asked each disciple to forsake the world (England) and go to Taos, New Mexico with him. Middleton Murry refused to go, but kissed Lawrence. Ners Catherine Carswell implied that Murray had betrayed Lawrence. Murry reportedly answered, "I *have* betrayed you, old chap, and I confess it." Then "Lawrence put his head on the table and vomited. The disciples, including Judas, raised 'the limp figure of their master' and took him home."[6] For natural inspiration, Lawrence, much influenced by Mme. Blavatsky and the idea of the cow as a sacred object in nature-based religions, saw the cow as a symbol of Isis. In Taos, Lawrence met his sacred cow, Susan, whom he looked on with reverence, saying, "[i]s not this my life, this throbbing of the bull's blood

---

[5.] See Esther Shephard, *Walt Whitman's Pose* (New York: Harcourt, Brace, 1938); and Frances Winwar, *The Life of the Heart, George Sand and Her Times* (New York: Harper & Brothers, 1945), 214, 247, 286.

[6.] William York Tindall, *D.H. Lawrence and Susan His Cow* (New York: Columbia University Press, 1939), 24.

in my blood?" He was here recalling the Mithraic bull.[7]
Perhaps Susan helps explain why in *Lady Chatterly's Lover*,
Lawrence presents anal sexual intercourse as the ultimate
pleasure.

Many other names from the literary, political, and
intellectual worlds could be cited as instances of this
pronounced will to fiction in the modern world. Nietzsche,
because of his transvaluation of all values, had defended the lie
as pragmatically more valuable at times than the truth. This
spirit of pragmatism with respect to truth, or instrumentalism
with John Dewey, meant in essence that truth is what works.
For all too many, this instrumentalism came to mean that
truth is what works in my mind, to allay my fears or satisfy my
ego. This mental will to fiction has meant the proliferation of
"mental illness" and of psychology to cope with that mental
flight from reality.

Ludwig Feuerbach (1804-1872), in *The Essence of Christianity*
(1841), as a militant humanist, reduced religion to a theogonic
wish, the desire to bring God into existence. Man, he held,
cannot transcend his own being, and he creates a God-idea in
his own image. God is thus a wish-fulfillment idea, a projection
of man's nature and ideals. The "truth" of religion for
Feuerbach is that it is an expression of man's various ideals: its
falsity is that it tries to establish a god in order to admit the
validity of human ideals.

In *The Essence of Faith According to Luther* (1844), Feuerbach
held that the real motive of Christian belief in God is self-love
or human egoism. He declared, "God is a word the sole
meaning of which is 'man.'"[8] His summary of his thesis stated:

> I have shown you (in *The Essence of Christianity*) that the
> Supreme Object, which you find and believe is in your
> God, is the love of man for man. In doing so, I have taken
> care of you and your God inadequately. But that is not
> enough for you. You want to believe in something separate

---

7. *Ibid.*, 110; cf. 7, 3, 29, 84, 123f., 159-161, 178, 181, 192, 200.
8. Ludwig Feuerbach, *The Essence of Faith According to Luther* (New York: Harper & Row, 1967), 50.

from yourselves, something ineffable. But what is this thing you distinguish from love? It is your dear ego, which distinguished itself from love and is concerned only with itself. This love is merely your morality; but your religion, your essence, your God, is self-love. But if you insist on denying this, then find the determining factor and the final goal of your life attained in love, and give up your immoral self. But by "love" I mean activity of body and soul—living for others, for humanity, for universal ends. But since these universal ends only find actuality and truth in concrete human form (for example, if I want freedom, I want really free men; I do not want freedom merely thought about or intended; I want a visible and tangible freedom), I always frankly posit man as the alpha and omega.[9]

Man's "ideals" have not survived Feuerbach's abandonment of God, but man's self-love has, and it has increased. Feuerbach's philosophy was really an expression of the old Cainitic wish for the death of God, and it has led instead to the immanent death of humanistic culture. Feuerbach reduced theology to anthropology, but, without God, anthropology lost all content or essence, as a later existentialist, Sartre, was to make clear. The fiction motivating Feuerbach and his successors is that they move into freedom, even as they put on the chains of slavery. Freud furthered Feuerbach's thesis and identified *the will to live* with the *id, the pleasure principle*, the urge to parricide, incest, and cannibalism; whereas *the reality principle* was identified with the *ego, the will to death*, the inhibitory factor. The definition of the will to live in the post-Freudian era is thus closely allied to the will to fiction. Reality inhibits, because moral considerations and reality factors impose a brake on the pleasure principle. The answer, then, is away with the brakes. To cite an instance of this, medical literature gives abundant evidence of the serious genetic consequences of incest.[10] In spite of this, an increasing number of persons

---

9. *Ibid.*, 18f.
10. See for a summary, R.J. Rushdoony, *The Institutes of Biblical Law* (Nutley, NJ: The Craig Press, 1974), 368-375.

chooses to deny the evidence of genetic damage in the name of sexual freedom. Those who insist on denying the evidence include medical men.[11] The will to fiction, the insistence that sexual freedom must not be adversely affected by material factors, is very strong in such men.

The will to fiction governs political life, and sins like *envy* are dignified into heroic virtues by being given another name, called the demand for *social justice* and *equality*.[12] Unlike any other age, ours is saturated with fiction as entertainment: opera, the novel, radio, motion picture films, television, magazine stories, and the like. Children's minds are stuffed with hours of television fiction daily, and life becomes more fiction than reality to them. There is a very real connection between the old movies seen by children in the 1950s and the student riots of the 1960s as well as the hippie movement. The saturation with fiction is a product of the modern age and its philosophy. The area of certainty is the mind and imagination of man; the real world is a probability concept which daily recedes before the mind of modern man, whose imagination, geared to the pleasure principle, steadily cuts the ties to reality. For such people, reality has a habit of returning in the form of judgment and death.

[11.] See, for example, Martin Shephard, M.D., "The Urge to Incest," *Gallery* 2, no. 6 (June 1974): 96ff.

[12.] See Helmut Schoeck, *Envy, A Theory of Social Behavior* (New York: Harcourt, Brace & World, 1970).

9

From God to Nothingness

The validation of society in the Medieval Age was provided by God, whose authoritative voice was held to be the church, which through the popes, bishops, and priests instructed the people. It was the successful claim of the early emperors of the Holy Roman Empire that they were the authoritative voice of God, and the major conflict of the medieval centuries was with respect to the *transmission* of divine authority, whether by means of church or empire, to the nobility and the people.

With the Renaissance, the claim of the church was implicitly denied, as was that of the empire to a degree, in favor of kings in the practical realm, and autarchic man in the realm of theory. The Reformation and Counter-Reformation both reasserted the claims of the church in varying forms; but, with the rise of the Enlightenment, and then the age of pietistic withdrawal of Christians from the world, an essentially Deistic idea of God was seen as the initiator of the universe and of authority, which now resided in essence with "The People." Subsequently, the age of revolution and of humanistic sciences eliminated God entirely, so that man stood at the apex of the universe, with animals, plants, and inanimate matter under man.[1]

But, as we have seen, at the same time, modern man was denying meaning to the universe around him and reducing it to nothingness. Existential man stands alone, without essence, in a universe without essence, pattern, or meaning. Because all things are without meaning for modern man, he is past salvation, since salvation is *from something into something*, from sin into grace for the Christian. Where all the alternatives are *nothing*, no salvation is possible until meaning occurs.

Thus, as modern man and his culture decline into a deeper loss of meaning, the alternative to salvation becomes therapy for the dying. Rieff has said:

> Where family and nation once stood, or Church and Party, there will be hospital and theater too, the normative institutions of the next culture…. Religious man was born to be saved; psychological man is born to be pleased. The difference was established long ago, when 'I believe,' theory of the ascetic, lost precedence to 'one feels,' the caveat of the therapeutic. And if the therapeutic is to win out, then surely the psychotherapist will be his secular spiritual guide.[2]

In a world of nothingness, however, the very idea of *health* becomes impossible. In a world without meaning, neither health nor sickness can be defined. Freud thus promised no healing, only a reconciliation with our condition, so that therapy is the acceptance of our condition.[3]

The modern temper is thus what Michael Novak calls "the experience of nothingness." It is a denial of all meaning in favor of life by myth, life by recognition that meaning is impossible and that truth does not exist in a void.

---

[1] For a somewhat varying but essentially similar analysis, see Eugene A. Nide, *Religion Across Culture* (New York: Harper & Row, 1968), 48-57.

[2] Philip Rieff, *The Triumph of the Therapeutic: Uses of Faith After Freud* (New York: Harper & Row, 1966), 24f.

[3] See R.J. Rushdoony, *Freud* (Nutley, NJ: Presbyterian & Reformed Publishing Co., 1973).

Descartes began with the autonomous mind or self as his solid core of reality. Novak can allow no reality, no meaning:

> I am not a self, never did possess a self, do not have a permanent and indestructible identity, and have no special need to mourn its absence.... The self has no pure identity, substance, core of its own; it is constituted by activities in engagement with the world. There is no self over and apart from the world. There is only a self *in the world, part of the world, in tension with the world, resistant to the world.* It would be better (although after so many centuries our language scarcely would allow it), to drop the expression "self" entirely, and to speak instead of "a conscious world" or, indeed, "a horizon." I am a conscious world, a horizon, a two-poled organism, a conscious, open-ended, protean structuring of a world. The world exists through my consciousness and my consciousness through it: not two, but one-in-act.[4]

When Novak speaks to an audience, he feels "the ocean as myself." He finds that we are a "we." "When you attend to me, you make me exist for you."[5] What then is the experience of nothingness? It is the recognition that all our ideas which order our lives and experiences are myths and can never be more than myths, because existence has no meaning, goal, or end. In the place of Descartes's myth, "I *think*, therefore I am," Novak declares that a new affirmation, present in the growing subculture, is simply, "I *feel*."[6] To *feel* is simply *to respond* to the stimuli of the world, and, Novak writes, "[t]he self is a recipient of stimuli in a darkened room."[7]

The result is the loss of all meaning. This places Novak in the position of being compelled, and to his credit is his honesty, to face the issue: Hitler shared the same affirmation of nothingness, as did Mussolini, "self-confessed nothingness, not merely of a literary sort." His answer to the similarity of beliefs is inadequate: "Hitler forced men to distinguish

---

[4.] Michael Novak, *The Experience of Nothingness* (New York: Harper & Row, 1970), 55.
[5.] *Ibid.*, 56.
[6.] *Ibid.*, 5.
[7.] *Idem.*

between the experience of nothingness, which is human and valid, and nihilism, which draws from that experience corrupting, inhumane, and indefensible conclusions."[8] Novak's starting point, nothingness, gives him no ground for distinguishing between his ideas and Hitler's. His "humane" ideas are borrowed from the heritage of Catholic faith; they are not the logical conclusions of the experience of nothingness. The experience of nothingness means the end of meaning and of judgment, the end of the ability to differentiate and to discriminate. Only feeling, sensation, remains, in a void.

After the pattern of Tillich, Novak holds:

> *Granted that I am empty, alone, without guides, direction, will, or obligations, how shall I live?* In the nothingness, one has at least an opportunity to shape one's own identity, to create oneself. The courage to accept despair becomes the courage to be.[9]

The courage to be what? Nothing: simply to be. As we have seen, Sartre holds that it makes no difference whether one becomes a drunkard or a head of state. The drunkard is somewhat favored as more existential in his being. "The courage to be" in Tillich and Novak is simply the illogical insistence that continued existence after the experience of nothingness is somehow a virtue. But virtue, in their world, does not exist, and the whole of the existentialist's "courage" is simply an ignoble retreat from the challenge of reality into the neutral and undemanding nature of nothingness.

The champions of the experience of nothingness are at least more honest than most modern theologians, in that they have pushed the denial of the triune God nearly to its logical epistemological conclusion: no God, no man, *nothing*. To abandon the triune God of Scripture and His infallible word is ultimately to abandon all things, to abandon meaning for nothingness. Modern man has retreated into nothingness in his

---

8. *Ibid.*, 51f.
9. *Ibid.*, 61.

flight from God. Even there, however, all things are unendurable, and modern man is haunted by dreams of terror, unreason, and destruction, because, having fled from God, he flees also from God's creation, which includes his own being. To flee from God to nothingness is to run headlong into judgment. Philosophy becomes pretension and evasion, and man's despair a façade for his willful sin.

10

A Note on Earthquakes, Volcanoes, and Women

The Enlightenment's deification of Reason had important consequences for women: it meant their progressive subjugation to men in an anti-Biblical sense, and their separation from the world of affairs. In the medieval and Reformation eras, the role of women in society was a *necessary* one. While their position was held to be in subordination to their fathers and then their husbands, it was not one of irrelevance. A wife was to her husband what a prime minister is to a king, only stronger, in that she could not be dismissed as a prime minister can be. The practical and usually theoretical role of women was thus a very important one.

With the Enlightenment, men with amazing arrogance saw themselves as *rational* creatures, and women as merely *emotional* creatures. Clearly, authority could not be given to passion, and as a result, the control and possession of property and power by women was steadily limited and/or denied. Progress was held to require the rule of Reason, meaning the male. Passion would thereby be rendered harmless, and the world would advance more rapidly towards utopia.

Whatever is, is right, the Enlightenment proclaimed, and it was right that women, representing passion, be regarded as fit only for those duties pertaining to children and religion, and not for the pursuit of ideas. Thus began the long association of women with church life which marks the modern era. Religion, it was held, as it appears in the churches, is not rational; its appeal is thus essentially to women and children. Reason governs the world of Nature and must govern the world of men.

An earthquake shattered this superficial rationale and changed the thinking of the Western world: on November 1, 1775, 15,000 people lost their lives in the Lisbon earthquake. Its intellectual repercussions exceeded its physical damage. Rational religion, philosophy, and art began to crumble, and the Romantic movement was born in a generation. As Kendrick observed of the men of that day, "[a]fter the earthquake they were not going to admit that everything that happens, happens for the best, that whatever is, is right."[1] The totally rational God of the philosophers, the first cause who was also the Great Mathematician, had suddenly been revealed as irrational. Whether called God or Nature, the Enlightenment idea of the ultimate was suddenly irrelevant to reality. Instead of being "the best of all possible worlds," the world was suddenly alien to all such concepts and oblivious to Man's idea of reason. Clark has observed:

> Readers of Voltaire's *Candide* will remember how the smooth surface of commonsense optimism was cracked by the Lisbon earthquake of 1755. It was the eighteenth-century equivalent of the sinking of the *Titanic*. The immediate effect of the earthquake was extraordinary. Madame de Pompadour gave up rouge for a week ('she has offered it up,' said Horace Walpole, 'to the Demon of Earthquakes') and for a fortnight the stakes wagered at White's were substantially reduced. 'Never before,' said Goethe (who was six at the time), 'has the Demon of Fear so quickly and so powerfully spread horror throughout the land.'[2]

[1.] T.D. Kendrick, *The Lisbon Earthquake* (Philadelphia, PA: J.B. Lippincott Co., 1955), 179.

For humanistic man, the setting at naught of all human calculations and philosophies meant that the universe had to be irrational. God and reason had been defined, together with nature, in terms of man, in terms of man's image of himself. Any contradictions of that image meant that God and nature were irrational.

A major consequence of this change was a changed view of women. Irrationality, not reason, was now ultimate and omnipotent. The Romantics thus regarded women as a potential goddesses or potential witches. Enlightenment man could call a woman a goddess, but it was self-serving flattery, and a part of courtly etiquette, not reality. The goddesses of art were alluring beauties whose function it was to please the males gods, and no more.

Now woman became as fearful a power as dark and irrational nature, ever a potential earthquake or volcanic eruption. Man could only live with this irrationality by circumspection, working ever to keep it under the control of male reason. Increasingly, the emphasis of this new movement was on "the natural superiority of women."

Men, too, began to abandon reason, especially after Freud, and sought to gain power through primitivism and irrationality. Liberal males began to imitate women in their ostensible hyper-emotionalism, and to wear their hair long, as a sign of their loss of rationalistic inhibitions. Conservative males, in contrast, acted as Enlightenment men of Reason, called to suppress and put into its place that mass of irrationality known as woman.

Society was acting out a role in a drama of social roles written by the logic of modern philosophy.

We should not be surprised by this. Men commit suicide even when their outward circumstances invite envy from others, because their imaginations are filled with obsessive and

---

2. Kenneth Clark, *The Romantic Rebellion* (New York: Harper & Row, 1973), 45.

perverse ideas. The suicide is killed by his mind, by his ideas. Societies are no less victims of their own imagination.

Power in the Modern World

Power and Meaning

"Power is the name of the game," according to a popular adage, and there is more than a little truth to this statement. Before analyzing *the meaning of power*, and *the power of meaning*, it is important to define the term *power*. Western civilization has long been heavily influenced by the muddy waters of Aristotle's thought, and one of the greatest influences exercised by Aristotle has been on the idea of power. Stokes has observed that "later writers, as Hobbes and Locke, have done little more than repeat Aristotle."[1] Aristotle wrote:

> Clearly, then, in one sense the potentiality for acting and being acted upon is one (for a thing is "capable" both because it itself possesses the power of being acted upon, and also because something else has the power of being acted upon by it); and in another sense it is not; for it is partly in the patient (for it is because it contains a certain principle, and because even the matter is a kind of principle, that the patient is acted upon by another: oily stuff is inflammable, and stuff which yields in a certain way is breakable, and similarly in other cases)—and partly

---

[1] George J. Stokes, "Power," in James Hastings, editor, *Encyclopaedia of Religion and Ethics*, vol. 10 (Edinburgh: T. & T. Clark, 1930), 143.

in the agent; *e.g.*, heat and the art of building: the former in that which produces heat, and the latter in that which builds. Hence in so far as it is a natural unity, nothing is acted upon by itself; because it is one, and not a separate thing. "Incapacity" and "the incapable" is the privation contrary to "capacity" in this sense; so that every "capacity" has a contrary incapacity for producing the same result in respect of the same subject....

Since some of these principles are inherent in inanimate things, and other in animate things and in the soul in the rational part of the soul, it is clear that some of the potencies also will be irrational and some rational. Hence all arts, *i.e.*, the productive sciences, are potencies; because they are principles of change in another thing, or in the artist himself *qua* other.[2]

Potency or power can thus mean several things: the power to produce change, to be changed, to resist change, or to be an agency of change. Implicit in this is not only the fact that power is inescapably tied to change, but also that the ability to change and/or control others is the epitome of power, for to change others requires greater power than to be changed by them. The mainstream of Western civilization is thus apparent, the desire to control and change others as the essence of true power. This lust for power, the pathology of all fallen men, is common to cultures all over the world. It is an expression of man's original sin, his desire to be as God, knowing or determining for himself what constitutes good and evil (Genesis 3:5). This sin, the great temptation and the mainspring of the Fall, has, among other things, two facets. *First*, to be as God, or every man his own god, means a claim to autonomy, ultimacy, and power by the creature. Adam and Eve understood power as the ability to rebel against the authority of God and to destroy, by a positive act of disobedience, the order of Eden. The power to create or build is at best slow and laborious for man; the power to destroy is immediate, and consequently best expresses the lust for power.

[2.] Aristotle, *The Metaphysics, Books 1-9* (London: William Heinemann, 1956), 431f.

As George Orwell saw, in *1984*, the urge to power finally becomes nothing more than the sadistic image of a boot grinding down a human face. The most common expressions of power among fallen men are the urge to rebellion and destruction. The lust for power in fallen man is pathological, because for him the meaning of power or change is rebellion and destruction. Revolutionary movements in the modern world have thus been, as Jacques Ellul has seen, forces for reaction, because the changes they institute are destructive and regressive.

Second, the Fall was a claim by man to define good and evil autonomously, in terms of himself. It was a claim to the power of meaning, the power to define, to be the yardstick in terms of which reality is to be judged. All things are made relative to autonomous man and his will as the principle of definition. Because meaning and definition are made relative to man rather than God, they change as man changes. Situation ethics makes morality relative to man, because man is the new absolute and the source of all definition. In Scripture, ethics is relative to God, who is the source of all meaning, and man, as a creature, must conform to the absolute law of the absolute God. The power of meaning in Scripture belongs entirely to God who is the only source of definition and interpretation, and the only source of power. According to David, "God hath spoken once; twice have I heard this; that power belongeth unto God" (Psalm 62:11). Moreover, with respect to all powers within the universe, they are derivative. According to St. Paul, there is no power but of God: "the powers that be are ordained of God" (Romans 13:1). Not only power but also meaning is derivative. The God who created all things is the only source of their meaning and interpretation. God Himself is beyond definition.

This was clearly set forth to Moses:

> 13. And Moses said unto God, Behold, when I come unto the children of Israel, and shall say unto them, The God of your fathers hath sent me unto you; and they shall say to me, What is his name? what shall I say unto them?

14. And God said unto Moses, I AM THAT I AM: and he said, Thus shalt thou say unto the children of Israel, I AM hath sent me unto you.

15. And God said moreover unto Moses, Thus shalt thou say unto the children of Israel, The LORD God of your fathers, the God of Abraham, the God of Isaac, and the God of Jacob, hath sent me unto you: this is my name for ever, and this is my memorial unto all generations. (Exodus 3:13-15)

Moses, asking for God's name, asked God to define Himself; the experience of the centuries was baffling to Moses, and the God of his fathers (Exodus 3:6) was incomprehensible to him. The long silence, and the years of suffering, raised questions in Moses' mind: he wanted an easily defined God, one who by definition would be known and could be useful in terms of it. God, however, refused to be defined: I am He Who Is, the self-existent one, the creator, the source of all meaning and definition, God declared. Then, having made it clear that He was beyond definition, being the source of all definition, the ultimate and uncreated being, God described Himself as the God of the patriarchs, the God who reveals Himself. Again and again, Scripture makes clear that, while *God cannot be defined*, being beyond definition by anything outside of Himself, and beyond limitation, since definitions set limits, *God can still be described by His self-revelation*. In essence, the description the Scriptures give of God is an historical description: God is described by His acts. Attributes of God are also cited in Scripture: thus, we are told that "God is love" (1 John 4:8). This cannot be called a definition of God, because, while God is love, He is also more than love; He is more than His attributes.

Christianity today, being largely infected by humanism, fails too often to see that God is the only source of all power and meaning. Too often power is associated in pagan terms with social control and change, rather than with God, in whom power is inseparable from His holiness and righteousness.

God's revelation of Himself is given to man infallibly in His word, but is present, although sinful man cannot interpret it apart from the Scriptures, nor interpret it infallibly even then, in all His handiwork, in all creation. "The heavens declare the glory of God; and the firmament sheweth his handiwork" (Psalm 19:1). Man himself, as a creature made in the image of God, is a revelational fact: God's image in man is a witness to the nature of God and is descriptive in part of God, of His communicable attributes. We are told in Scripture that, basic to the image of God in man (Genesis 1:27), is *knowledge* (Colossians 3:10, "put on the new man, which is renewed in knowledge after the image of him that created him"); *righteousness and holiness* (Ephesians 4:24, "put on the new man, which after God is created in righteousness and true holiness"); and *dominion* (Genesis 1:28, "And God blessed them: and God said unto them, Be fruitful, and multiply, and replenish the earth, and subdue it; and have dominion over the fish of the sea, and the fowl of the air, and over every living thing that moveth upon the earth"). The image of God in man means also that the law of God is written in man's heart (Romans 2:14).

Change, or the ability to change, is identified as *power* in pagan thought. This meaning does not appear in the Biblical doctrine of power. God identifies Himself as the one who is beyond change, "For I am the LORD, I change not" (Malachi 3:6), but He does not go on to speak of Himself as the one who causes change; there are incidental references to this fact, that it is God who brings change to pass, but it is not made central to Scripture. The power of God is set forth, in this area, as *creative and regenerative*, and regeneration is far greater in scope than bare change. Moreover, Scripture makes clear *the inability of man to change essentials*: "Can the Ethiopian change his skin, or the leopard his spots? then may ye also do good, that are accustomed to do evil" (Jeremiah 13:23). Moreover, Solomon declared:

> 21. My son, fear thou the LORD and the king: and meddle not with them that are given to change.
> 22. For their calamity shall rise suddenly; and who knoweth the ruin of them both? (Proverbs 24:21-22).

Because of the nexus of knowledge, righteousness, holiness, and dominion in man because of God's image, it means that the Biblical doctrine of power requires the unity of these things. Regeneration is reserved to God; the power given to man is tied up with dominion, and true dominion is inseparable from knowledge, righteousness, and holiness. It is not accidental that knowledge has been most developed in Christian cultures and has been basic to dominion, *i.e.*, it has had a practical character and has been related to godly rule to a great degree. Knowledge in other cultures has too often replaced action and has been theoretical and hence abstract in relations to history and power. The modern trend towards knowledge for knowledge's sake is a return to paganism.

Too often, of course, not only pagan history but also the history of ostensibly Christian realms has been largely infected by the pagan doctrine of power as the ability to change or to control others. With the revival of pagan thought in the Enlightenment, such a doctrine of power led logically to *revolution*. In Hobbes, Locke, and their successors, power became simply the ability to control and to bring about changes via control. The goal of enlightened man became change, and the power to effect change. The humanistic millennium was to be ushered in, as Bredvold noted, *first*, by "the rejection of history, of the inheritance from the past." *Second*, this goal meant wiping the slate clean and beginning all over again. All past institutions and customs must be discarded and destroyed. *Third*, evil was held to be in the environment, not in man, so that social improvement should be directed, not against a supposed evil in human nature, but against the evil in the environment. *Fourth*, it was held that "by changing human institutions human nature itself will be born again."[3] A Soviet Russian philosopher, I. K. Luppol, has given a modern statement of this same faith, declaring:

[3.] Louis I. Bredvold, *The Brave New World of the Enlightenment* (Ann Arbor, MI: University of Michigan Press, 1961), 112f.

Are the morals of a nation bad? The cause is bad laws, a deplorable form of government. To improve the manners and morals it is therefore necessary to change the structure of the state. This is the aspect of the social doctrine of French materialism which Karl Marx had in mind when he wrote that eighteenth-century materialism leads directly to socialism and communism.... [I]t does not require much intelligence to grasp the connection between materialist doctrine on the one hand, a doctrine which teaches the innate tendency of man to goodness, the equality of intellectual aptitudes among all men, the omnipotence of experience, habit, and education, the influence of external circumstances on a man's nature, etc., and on the other hand, communism and socialism.[4]

A *fifth* factor was also added as necessary to the establishment of this humanistic millennium, the new managers of society, the philosopher-kings, the scientific-socialist elite of the state.

The radical break with Biblical faith that this dream requires is an emphatic one. It is a return to the pagan dream of power. Let us remember that Zeus was a divinized hero, whose grave was known, and of whom the legends of Olympus spoke frankly as an immoral god. Power was thus amoral Olympian control in such a faith, and even the power of Zeus was limited, because, finally, *change* overwhelms all the gods. The morality of pagan doctrines of power must thus be relativistic and existential: it is a product of man and of his desires, and since his desires mean in large measure *power*, might makes right.

The Bible never asks us *to change men*: regeneration is the power reserved to God, and it surpasses change: it is a re-creation. What the Bible does require of us is that, having been made a new creation in Christ, we exercise anew the creation mandate of Genesis 1:26-28, to subdue the earth and to exercise dominion in every area of life and thought in knowledge, righteousness, and holiness. This calling of the Christian man to govern the world is underscored by St. Paul, who writes, "Do ye not know that the saints shall judge the world?" (1

---

4. Cited from I.K. Luppol, *Diderot, Ses Idees and Philosophiques* (1936), translated by Y. Feldman, in *ibid*, 114.

Corinthians 6:2). The church, St. Paul says, is a training ground to prepare the covenant man to *judge, i.e.,* to govern, to exercise dominion, over the world, in time and eternity.

Christian thought on the matter of godly dominion was crystallized by John Wyclif, who spoke of dominion in the full sense of *authority* and *ownership.* God is the universal lord or *dominus,* having absolute dominion over all things. All men, as God's creatures called to exercise dominion, hold all things they possess and are called to possess as a feudal grant from God, as a *beneficium.* Every *beneficium* implies and requires a corresponding *service* to God and to men under God and in terms of His law. Ungodly men, in revolt against God, fail to render their due service to God, and to men in God, to those above and below them, and as a result they have no *rightful* possession of anything, no rightful dominion.

The wicked thus have *godless power* but not dominion. The righteous have *dominion,* but not always full freedom to exercise their dominion. Nonetheless, Wyclif held, "[e]very righteous man is lord over the whole sensible world."[5]

The righteous cannot establish their dominion more fully by rebellion or revolution, for change is not regeneration, and *control is not dominion.* By using their every opportunity to extend their dominion, and by recognizing that the wages of sin is always death (Romans 6:23), and sinful power is suicidal, the godly must work to further their dominion and to claim every area of life and thought in terms of the crown rights of King Jesus. Christian reconstruction is thus their calling and duty.

Godly power is the exercise of knowledge, righteousness, and holiness to extend dominion (authority and ownership) in every area of life, to make every institution, nation, science, art, and activity an area of Christ's over-lordship. His great commission is thus to be understood in terms of Genesis 1:26-28, for Christ sends forth the regenerate and new humanity to exercise dominion in His name, saying:

[5.] John Wyclif, *De Civ. Dom.* i., chapts. 7, 14.

18. All power is given unto me in heaven and in earth.

19. Go ye therefore, and teach all nations, baptizing them in the name of the Father, and of the Son, and of the Holy Ghost:

20. Teaching them to observe all things whatsoever I have commanded you: and, lo, I am with you always, even unto the end of the world. Amen. (Matthew 28:18-20)

2

The Death of Man

In Genesis 2:17, God declared to Adam that, on the day that Adam disobeyed God and ate of the forbidden fruit, he would "surely die," or "dying, thou shalt die." In brief, the process of death would begin to work in Adam.

Let us now, at some length, analyze what this sentence of death meant and means. An insight into its meaning appears in Ephesians 3:15. Earlier, in Ephesians 2:18, God the Father is spoken of as "the Father" to whom believers have access by adoption in Christ. In chapter 3, verse 14, God the Father is spoken of as "the Father of our Lord Jesus Christ," and then follows, in verse 15, the statement concerning God, that He is the one "[o]f whom the whole family in heaven and earth is named." Some commentators would limit this "whole family" to "all races of the children of God who through Jesus Christ, not by nature, but through the new birth, were created in Christ Jesus, 2:10, and are now children of God."[1] This seems unduly to restrict the meaning of the text. There is another meaning which seems to fit more closely with the temper of

---

[1.] G. Stoeckhardt, *Commentary on St. Paul's Letter to the Ephesians,* translated by Martin S. Sommer (St. Louis, MO: Concordia, 1952), 168.

101

the passage, namely, that entrance into the faith is entrance into the true meaning of life, family, and all things else.

Westcott interpreted Ephesians 3:15 thus:

> The absolute title expresses an important truth. In pre-Christian times GOD had revealed Himself as Father to one race: now it is made known that all the races of men are bound to Him in Christ by a like connexion; and far more than this. He Who is the Father of men is also the source of fellowship and unity in all the orders of finite being. The social connexions of earth and heaven derive their strength from Him; and represent under limited conditions the power of His Fatherhood....
>
> Every 'family', every society which is held together by the tie of a common head and author of its being, derives that which gives it a right to the title from the one Father. From Him comes the spirit by which the members have fellowship one with another and are all brought together into a supreme unity.[2]

Just as God is the creator of all reality, so, too, God is the primary reality. Apart from Him, nothing can exist. All justice, order, structure, design, and righteousness come from Him. (Evil is man's rebellion against God and God's order.) All things, all families, all structures are *named*, or take their names, from God. As we have seen, names in the Bible are definitions. *When St. Paul says of God that it is He "of whom the whole family in heaven and earth is named," he means thereby that all things receive their structure, design, meaning, and purpose from God and have none apart from Him.* Every aspect of life is *named* by God, is defined and can only be lived and understood in terms of Him.

Thus, any attempt by man, in rebellion against God, to maintain civil order, family life, community, or anything else apart from God is doomed. The more men and cultures abandon God and His law-word, the more they forsake life in all its forms.

[2.] Brooke Foss Westcott, *Saint Paul's Epistle to the Ephesians* (Grand Rapids, MI: William B. Eerdmans, 1952), 50.

There is thus no community in hell, no family life, no unity, no relationships, nothing but total isolation in hell. The imagery of hell in Scripture emphasizes this fact of total isolation: weeping, wailing, and gnashing of teeth, the self-torment of the isolated and totally self-absorbed; there is also the imagery of fire, and the gnawing worm, the burning of conscience and sterile remorse, total dedication to self-exaltation with total self-pity. Separation from God is thus hell and the death of man.

As we have seen, the pagan and humanistic view of power is power as the ability to control and change others. Unlike God, man cannot regenerate, he cannot make man anew from within, and as a result he strives to coerce man into the desired patterns. The result is disillusionment. Whether the *philosophes* of the Enlightenment or the revolutionists and liberals of the nineteenth and twentieth centuries, humanistic reformers have found men resistant to their proposed changes. Coercion only breeds sullen resistance. Hence, very early, a central aspect of the humanistic faith came to be *a hatred for man as he is.* Friedrich Nietzsche carried this position to its logical conclusion. Beginning with the love of man, he turned on humanity for rejecting his "reforms" and answers. The need is not for man, but for superman, and superman can only be born if man is destroyed. Humanity must be smashed and remolded in order to create a super-race. The world of the future is to be beyond good and evil, beyond morality, and also beyond man. Since Nietzsche's superman is at war with God and with man alike, he is, Nietzsche conceded, perhaps most clearly to be identified as the devil:

> Zarathustra, the first psychologist of the good man, is consequently the friend of the evil man. When a degenerate man arises to the highest rank, he must do so only at the cost of the reverse type—at the cost of the strong man who is certain of life. When the herd-animal shines with the bright rays of the purest virtue, the exceptional man must be degraded to the rank of the evil. When falsehood insists at all costs on claiming the word "truth" as its world-outlook, the really truthful man must

be sought out among those of worst repute. Zarathustra is quite equivocal here; he says that it was precisely the knowledge of the good, of the "best," that caused his horror of men. And it was out of this feeling of repulsion that he grew the wings with which to soar into distant futures. He does not conceal the fact that this type of man, a relatively superhuman type, is superhuman particularly as compared with the "good" man, and that the good and the just would call his superman the *devil*.[3]

Here, as in other passages, the truth comes out. There is no superman in Nietzsche, no new life beyond good and evil. Nietzsche's superman is also a negation and a destroyer, and he rightly describes this type of man as the devil. Nietzsche cannot affirm life in the end, nor community, nor love, nor anything except hatred, destruction, and self-isolation. His thinking, and that of all his fellow atheists, made Orwell's *1984* a logical conclusion. Orwell saw the end result of the modern dream of power:

> Power is in inflicting pain and humiliation. Power is in tearing human minds to pieces and putting them together again in new shapes of your own choosing. Do you begin to see, then, what kind of world we are creating? It is the exact opposite of the stupid hedonistic Utopias that the old reformers imagined. A world of fear and treachery and torment, a world of trampling and being trampled upon, a world which will grow not less but *more* merciless as it refines itself. Progress in our world will be progress toward more pain. The old civilizations claimed that they were founded on love and justice. Ours is founded upon hatred.... If you want a picture of the future, imagine a boot stamping on a human face—forever.[4]

This is the necessary goal of the pagan dream of power. Because man is created in God's image, he can never be successfully made over into man's planned image. The result is frustration for power-motivated man, and, in his anger, he employs all his

---

[3.] Friedrich Nietzsche, "'Ecce Homo,' Why I am a Fatality," in *The Philosophy of Nietzsche* (New York: Modern Library, n.d.), 138f.
[4.] George Orwell, *1984* (New York: Signet, 1951), 203.

power all the more nakedly in order to use man as his total creature, and to do so destructively.

In the process of arriving at this goal, humanistic man must eliminate Biblical moral considerations from the human scene. Biblical morality affirms that all absolute power belongs to God, and that man's power is a gift and a blessing. The gift is withdrawn as man's moral obedience to God declines. In Deuteronomy 28, we have an emphatic statement on the correlation of morality with blessings and power. Gifts are withdrawn where disobedience prevails, and power is transferred to the faithful and obedient.

As against this, the humanist must insist that moral judgments cannot be used, because they intrude a supposedly private and discriminatory judgment. Dr. Basile Yanovsky, in his record of work in a New York venereal disease clinic, reports on a complaint filed against him. In treating a seventeen-year-old girl, he had concluded his check-up with the words, "And meanwhile, behave!" This was grounds for a complaint against him of violating the patient's privacy. In a world of crime, corruption, and disease, Dr. Yanovsky noted, the intolerable fact was a moral world![5] The sick world of disease and crime cannot permit moral judgment, because it then stands condemned and powerless. If the validity of moral judgment in terms of God's word is recognized, then the entire fabric of the modern world can only be self-condemned.

It stands, of course, condemned in God's sight, but its collapse would come more quickly if it stood condemned in its own eyes. Some of the death of God thinkers have seen their philosophy as requiring as its consequence the death of man.[6] To abandon God and His law is for man on any terms to abandon life as well.

According to Deuteronomy 28:2 and 15, irresistible blessings follow obedience to God's law, and irresistible curses

---

[5.] Dr. Basile Yanovsky, M.D., *The Dark Side of Venus, From a Doctor's Log-book* (New York: Harcourt Brace Jovanovich, 1973), 240.
[6.] See R.J. Rushdoony, *The Word of Flux* (Fairfax, VA: Thoburn Press, 1975).

follow disobedience.[7] The curse that began with the Fall pursues man into death and hell. The blessing of God through Christ means the beginning of a new creation, and the triumph of man in and through Him.

[7.] See R.J. Rushdoony, *The Institutes of Biblical Law* (Nutley, NJ: The Craig Press, 1973), 660-664.

3

Godly Rule

Salvation means very different things to different people and to different cultures. It is thus unwise to talk about salvation unless we are specific as to its meaning. When Peter spoke about salvation, he spoke to the men of Israel, whose knowledge of the meaning salvation was specific and extensive, but, even then, Peter was careful to give a full statement. The inspired summary of his statement tells us:

> 10. Be it known unto you all, and to all the people of Israel, that by the name of Jesus Christ of Nazareth, whom ye crucified, whom God raised from the dead, even by him doth this man stand here before you whole.
> 11. This is the stone which was set at nought of you builders, which is become the head of the corner.
> 12. Neither is there salvation in any other: for there is no other name under heaven given among men, whereby we must be saved. (Acts 4:10-12)

Twice Peter cites the *name*, the definition of salvation, as *Jesus Christ* and all that He was and especially did, *i.e.*, His atonement and resurrection. He thus defined salvation as the person and work of Jesus Christ.

Very different ideas of salvation were then current in the empire. The imperial salvation was a system of cradle to grave security and care which was actually serfdom. Serfdom originated in this imperial plan, when men traded freedom for security on imperial estates. As Ramsay wrote, "[t]hus serfdom became the goal of the imperial order, and produced the developed serfdom of the medieval land-system, which lasted in Russia until about 1869." The problems of freedom were gladly surrendered by many men for the security of slavery. As Ramsay summarized the issue:

> The logical issue of the paternal system of government as we see it fully carried out under the Roman Empire, was the negation of freedom. In its opposition to the imperial policy the religion of Christ was the champion of freedom. Such is its spirit in central Asia, where we can best see it, during the second century. Such is its spirit as declared by Paul to the people of Antioch, Iconium, etc.: "ye were called for freedom," and "for freedom did Christ set us free: stand fast therefore, and be not entangled again in a yoke of bondage" (Galatians v. 13 and 1). He spoke to nations of slaves, and the Phrygians and Lycaonians, raised in some small degree from the condition of slavery by the Graeco-Roman education, but liable to slip back again as the Imperial System developed its paternal character thoroughly. The "Salvation" of Jesus and of Paul was freedom: the "Salvation" of the Imperial system was serfdom.[1]

The pagan doctrine of salvation as economic security, and as slavery, is again very much with us, and the result is the messianic role of Marxism, Fabian Socialism, welfare democracies, fascism, and other social structures.

Another common error concerning salvation which prevailed then, and continues to prevail now was the identification of salvation with spirituality.[2] The material world was held to be, by neoplatonists and others, evil and

---

[1] Sir W.M. Ramsay, *The Bearing of Recent Discovery on the Trustworthiness of the New Testament* (London: Hodder and Stoughton, 1920), 197f.
[2] See R.J. Rushdoony, *The Flight From Humanity* (Nutley, NJ: The Craig Press, 1973).

fallen, and the spiritual world good. Salvation thus meant forsaking material things for things spiritual, and asceticism and flights from the world to the life of a hermit became common among pagans. These pagan movements exerted a deep influence on many Christians and led to the monastic movement, and, much later, to pietism. According to Scripture, however, man is totally fallen, in all his being, *i.e.*, the extent of the Fall affects every aspect of his being. The Fall is apparent in his "spirit" as much as in his "body." Man is a unity, and the Fall affected the whole man. There is no virtue inherent in either spirit or matter, nor any evil inherent in either. God made all things wholly good, and the Fall had its origin in the mind of man, so that the scholastic view (derived from Aristotle) that the mind is untainted by the Fall is clearly wrong. Satan is entirely a spiritual being; he is a creature, with a local being, but he is not a part of the material universe but of the angelic or spiritual order of beings. Satan as a spiritual creature is still fallen. The mind or spirit of man is not exempt from sin, and the more men have imagined that separation from the material world unto a spiritual or mental ivory tower constitutes virtue, the more they have blinded themselves to their sin.

Other ideas of salvation can be cited, but perhaps one more will suffice. For Buddhism and Hinduism, for example, *salvation is from life*. Life is the great evil, and the goal of reincarnation is to escape from life into everlasting death and nothingness. Thus, to offer a man salvation without being specific is dangerous. He may use Christ, as many have done and do, as the supposed means of delivering him his idea of salvation. It was because of this danger of misunderstanding that our Lord did not often speak openly of Himself as the Messiah. The element of doubt as to His nature and calling, and the intense excitement over His miraculous works, He used as opportunities to teach the people about the meaning of the Old Testament prophecies, so that they might see the savior and salvation in Scriptural terms. Israel, however, insisted on seeing the messiah as simply a greater David and no more, as a political ruler who would overthrow Rome and establish Israel as the world ruler.

It is thus essential to know what kind of salvation the Bible offers. According to W. Adams Brown's study, "[t]he root idea in salvation is *deliverance*," and "salvation is often used in the OT in the sense of 'victory.'" Successful warriors are called *saviors*, as in Judges 3:9, 15 and Nehemiah 9:27. Men are spoken of as saved also from troubles, death, enemies, violence, and reproach in the Old Testament. Healing, too, is cited as an aspect of salvation (James 5:16). God's "salvation brings with it not merely deliverance, but security and prosperity. This close connexion with prosperity is clearly brought out in such a passage as Psalm 118:25…(cf. Psalm 106:4-5)."[3] This salvation means deliverance now and at the end of the world. It is temporal and eternal, material and spiritual, personal and cosmic. *All things* will be made new. The great agent of this salvation, the only One who makes it possible, is the Messiah (Psalm 53:6, Isaiah 25:9; 45:8, 17; 46:13; 49:6, 25; 51:6; 56:1; 61:10; 62:11). Closely linked with this is the fact that judgment is a necessary part of salvation. We are judged, the world is judged, and the Messiah is both the Judge and the sin-bearer (Isaiah 53).

Israel, the covenant people of God by faith, shall be the world ruler. "As the condition of enjoying the future salvation is repentance on Israel's part (Isaiah 1:19-20), so it includes as one of its chief elements the righteousness of the nation (Jeremiah 31:31-34). The Messianic age is to be a time of justice and judgment and of the pure worship of God."[4]

The redeemed people of the Messiah will be a regenerated and greatly blessed people:

> 25. Then will I sprinkle clean water upon you, and ye shall be clean: from all your filthiness, and from all your idols, will I cleanse you.

---

[3] W. Adams Brown, "Salvation, Saviour," in James Hastings, editor, *A Dictionary of the Bible*, vol. 4 (New York: Charles Scribner's Sons, 1919), 357f.
[4] *Ibid.*, 359.

26. A new heart also will I give you, and a new spirit will I put within you: and I will take away the stony heart out of your flesh, and I will give you an heart of flesh.
27. And I will put my spirit within you, and cause you to walk in my statutes, and ye shall keep my judgments.
28. And ye shall dwell in the land that I gave to your fathers; and ye shall be my people, and I will be your God.
29. I will also save you from all your uncleannesses: and I will call for the corn, and will increase it, and lay no famine upon you.
30. And I will multiply the fruit of the tree, and the increase of the field, that ye shall receive no more reproach of famine among the heathen. (Ezekiel 36:25-30)

Among the promises of this declaration are, *first*, regeneration. The covenant people will be saved from their sins, and they will be made a new creation in the Lord. They will be "clean" before the Lord; they will have "a new heart," and God's Spirit will be within them. *Second*, they will keep the law of God and abide in terms of His statutes and judgments, so that, having been justified by the grace of God, they are now sanctified by the law. *Third*, they will receive material blessings, the land and good harvests, so that theirs is a happy and prosperous life.

Our Lord came as the bringer of salvation. St. Mark tells us, "Jesus came into Galilee, preaching the gospel of the kingdom of God, And saying, The time is fulfilled, and the kingdom of God is at hand: repent ye, and believe the gospel" (Mark 1:14f). Repentance and faith are required, and faith means to "believe the gospel," *i.e.*, Christ and His word and works in their totality. He is "the Kingdom of God at hand," present in Himself as the King, and as the one who, in the fulfilled time, makes all things new. By His resurrection, Jesus Christ, as the new Adam (1 Corinthians 15:45, 47), is the "firstfruits" of the new creation (1 Corinthians 15:20, 23).

In the apostolic preaching, "'Salvation' has become a technical term which sums up all the blessings brought by the Gospel" (Ephesians 1:13, 1 Corinthians 15:1f., Acts 13:26, etc.).[5] By His atonement and resurrection, Jesus Christ began

---

5. *Ibid.*, 365.

the recreation of all things, and the whole creation looks forward to the consummation of this deliverance (Romans 8:21, Colossians 1:20, Ephesians 1:10, 1 Corinthians 15:28).

Salvation in the Bible is essentially from *sin* and *death*, and all their consequences. It is both temporal and eternal, both individual and social, both present and future. It is the work of God through Christ to undo the fall of man and its consequences. Man was created to exercise dominion over the world as God's image bearer (Genesis 1:26-28). In Christ, man is restored to that calling. Salvation is the work of God: it is an act of sovereign grace. On the human side, man's response is *repentance, faith, and obedience. Regeneration is the beginning, and godly rule is the end of salvation.* St. Paul tells the Corinthians that they must learn to judge or govern their own affairs, because "the saints shall judge the world" (1 Corinthians 6:2). The word *judge* here means to administer the affairs of, and to govern. It is comparable to the Hebrew of the Book of Judges, as in Judges 3:10. The same Greek word appears in Matthew 19:28.

Regeneration is entirely the work of God. Man's duty is to proclaim the word of God and His regenerating power, and to bring all things into captivity to Christ, to exercise Godly rule.

It is an obvious fact that, if we claim to be Christians and continuously abide in adultery, and in dishonesty in our work, we are giving evidence not of faith but of unbelief. Our Lord *requires* us to judge in terms of His word, not ours: "Judge not according to the appearance, but judge righteous judgment" (John 7:24). "Ye shall know them by their fruits.... A good tree cannot bring forth evil fruit, neither can a corrupt tree bring forth good fruit.... Wherefore by their fruits ye shall know them" (Matthew 7:16, 18, 20).

We thus have an obligation to be holy, to be godly, to be law-abiding in terms of God's law-word, in our sexual and family life, and in our vocation. The church must be an area of holiness, but so too must the state and the school, the arts and the sciences, and all things else. Every area of life must be godly and must be made an aspect of the Kingdom of God.

A retreat from the responsibility of godly rule in any area is a retreat from the Biblical doctrine of salvation. Israel primarily expected political deliverance from the Messiah; the modern churchman expects little more than a spiritual deliverance. Both represent a perversion of the Scriptures.

The Christian must proclaim the fullness of salvation. He must declare the whole counsel of God, summon people to repentance, faith, and obedience. He must work to establish Christian churches, families, schools, civil governments, vocations, arts, and sciences. Because Christ is risen from the dead, our salvation is total in its extent. Had Christ's appearances after His death been ghostly appearances, then it would be necessary to limit our preaching to a purely spiritual and other-worldly victory. It would then be logical to say that, after being saved, little remains to the believer other than to rescue others and to wait for heaven.

But the Scriptures are emphatic: Christ arose from the dead in the self-same body in which He was crucified. The good news was and is the fact that all creation is being made new by Him who destroyed the power of sin and death. Christ sends us forth to conquer all men and nations (Matthew 28:18-20), and, at His coming again, the final enemy, all things else being subdued so that He reigns with all things under His feet, death itself shall be destroyed (1 Corinthians 15:25-27). This is *the victory* (1 Corinthians 15:57) that is ours in Christ.

Precisely because the early church did see salvation in its fullness, Rome waged war against it. It was Christ or Caesar: both claimed world rule and absolute power. Stauffer has summarized for us the Roman faith as expressed in the days of Augustus: "Salvation is to be found in none other save Augustus, and there is no other name given to men in which they can be saved. This is the climax of the Advent proclamation of the Roman empire."[6] Thus, when St. Peter on

---

6. Ethelbert Stauffer, *Christ and the Caesars* (Philadelphia, PA: Westminster Press, 1955), 88.

the day of the first confrontation of the apostles and the Sanhedrin, declared, "Neither is there salvation in any other: for there is none other name under heaven given among men, whereby we must be saved" (Acts 4:12), he was in effect challenging all the powers of the day with the exclusive saving power and lordship of Jesus Christ. This we must do once more. Jesus Christ was not offering and establishing by His sovereign grace a salvation like that of the mystery religions of His day, one for the soul alone, and other-worldly in essence. Neither was He offering political and economic security in the form of serfdom, as Rome was offering as salvation. As the Word of God, of whom the Scripture declares, "All things were made by him; and without him was not any thing made that was made" (John 1:3), He was reclaiming His creation, redeeming His elect, and establishing this world as His Kingdom. We dare not surrender the Crown Rights of King Jesus over a single inch of the universe, nor over any area of life and activity.

4

Power and the Law

In recent years, Northern Ireland has been the arena of a bitter and vicious conflict, ostensibly between Catholics and Protestants, but more probably between revolutionary and humanistic groups masquerading as religious causes. More than a few hundred have been murdered in this conflict. How deeply rooted is this strife? According to *British Record*,

> A public opinion poll conducted for the BBC in Northern Ireland shows that by an overwhelming majority—96 percent—the people of Northern Ireland of all Parties and shades of opinion reject the use of violence as a political weapon. Only 2 percent of those asked if they approved of violence for such purposes answered "yes."[1]

Some historians tell us that, despite the welfare mobs and the sexual revolutionaries in ancient Rome, most Romans before the fall of Rome were quiet, hard-working family men. Similar arguments for the basic stability of France before the Revolution, and of Russia before 1917, have been advanced. A very strong case can be made, in fact, for the freedom and progress of Russia, 1900-1917.

---

[1]. "Northern Ireland: Public Rejection of Violence," *British Record*, 6 (2 May 1974): 2.

Again, it can be pointed out that a larger number of revolutionists exist in the United States of 1974 than existed in old Russia and old France, although again it is a minority, albeit a powerfully active one.

However, it should be noted that the Puritans of the seventeenth century commanded England (and Europe diplomatically and militarily) while numbering only about four percent of the population.

Minorities can clearly dominate or take over a society, and they have done so repeatedly, but they can only do so if the faith of the overwhelming majority has eroded and is incapable of commanding others. When the majority has lost confidence in the power of their faith and morality to solve life's problems, or in the universal validity of what they believe, then power quickly slips from their grasp.

To cite a specific example, I believe that the overwhelming majority of Americans are against abortion. But abortion has become legal, without too great an outcry. Why? A doctor, personally against abortion, refused to come out against it because it meant "legislating for everybody." He saw his stand against abortion as a purely personal standard, not as a principle of universal validity. As a result, his ability to make a stand was severely limited. Similarly, many people who are against abortion have hesitated to oppose it, and have given favorable responses to surveys on the subject, because they believe that those who want it should have it, and "I don't have the right to legislate for everybody." For them, morality has become a matter of personal preference and taste, not a mandate from Almighty God.

The same is true of homosexuality. The overwhelming majority regard it with contempt and disgust, but again they hesitate to legislate against it. In speaking to Christian groups, I have often asked, after ascertaining the opposition of all present to homosexuality, how many favor the death penalty for it, as Scripture requires? I call attention to the key texts, Leviticus 20:13 and Romans 1:32, which give both Old and

New Testament authority to the penalty. I have not yet found any Christians who will assent to the death penalty. They disregard the Scriptures in order to plead humanistic considerations.

All this simply means that it is not the faith which now governs professing Christians, but statist humanism. Because God does not command them, they cannot command society, and small groups of strong though evil faith are able to disrupt society or to seize power.

Over and over again, Scripture declares that God has ordained that the consequences of sin are death, individually and culturally (Genesis 2:17, Deuteronomy 28:15ff.), whereas the consequences of faith and obedience are blessings and prosperity (Deuteronomy 28:1-14). The power of God's law is the power of the Almighty One. His decree to the wicked, both persons and nations, is "Thou shalt surely die," and if we Christians fail to declare this, God holds us accountable for their deaths (Ezekiel 3:18). Whatever the short-term advantage, in the long term, the wages of sin is always death (Romans 6:23).

Because this is God's principle of action, *first*, He requires that we adopt it as basic to the life of the state, the ministry of justice. Practically, this means protecting the law-abiding people of God from evil men and from all injustice. The state is required to be a ministry of justice, the protector of the good and a terror to the evil (Romans 13:1-7). Positively, this means the protection of the good, and the administration of justice in terms of God's word. Negatively, it means the death penalty. The death penalty for the lawless means life to the law-abiding. Not only is the death penalty required for murder and other crimes, but also for incorrigible delinquents and habitual offenders (Deuteronomy 21:18-21).[2] The death penalty is a theological principle which first appears in Genesis 2:17. God is the creator of all things, and life is only tenable in terms of

---

[2.] See R.J. Rushdoony, *The Institutes of Biblical Law* (Nutley, NJ: The Craig Press, 1974).

faith and obedience: man apart from God means man in total isolation and hell. "In him was life; and the life was the light of men" (John 1:4), we are told concerning God the Son. Only as men abide by faith and obedience in Christ, the creator and source of life, can they have life. Apart from Him, they perish under His judgment. We are told emphatically, "He that hath the Son hath life; and he that hath not the Son of God hath not life" (1 John 5:12). Because God is the Almighty One and the maker of all things, this declaration is not only true for theology but also for all of life, for every sphere of thought and activity. For the state or for the church to offer life to those who under God's law have forfeited it, is to sin grievously. There are not two kinds of truth, one valid in theology and another in politics and jurisprudence. We are not polytheists but Christians. Truth is one because God is one.[3] Thus, a first principle of godly power is to recognize that faith and obedience mean life, and sin and unbelief mean death.

Second, the law of God requires restitution (Exodus 22), and the goal of God's redemptive activity is the regeneration and restitution of all creation (Matthew 19:28, Acts 3:19-21). Jesus Christ came to make the only acceptable offering to God which could restore man from the death of sin to the life of righteousness. Fundamental to both God's plan of redemption and His laws for the state and society is restitution and restoration. It was basic to the Old Testament, and Zacchaeus spoke in terms of it when he pledged himself to fourfold restitution (Luke 19:8). When men, churches, families, and states make restitution basic to their standards, then and only then does godly justice prevail. The prison system is not a part of Scripture. The only function of prisons in Biblical law is to

---

3. In April, 1974, I was invited to speak for four Sunday nights at the Montecito Covenant Church, Santa Barbara, California, by the Rev. Bryan J.H. Leech. I spoke on April 21 and 28 on "Power and Meaning" and "The Death of Man." After the second evening, I was asked by a church officer if I believed in capital punishment, and I stated that I did. The two subsequent evening's studies in "Godly Rule" and "Power and the Law" were immediately cancelled.

hold a man in custody, pending trial. If guilty, he made restitution or worked out restitution as a bond servant, or, if guilty and a habitual criminal, he was executed as well, regardless of whether or not he could make restitution. Now, the man who is robbed is bereft of his possessions and is then taxed to support the thief in prison. Because God is One and His truth is one, restitution and restoration are God's principles not only for the plan of salvation, but also for justice in everyday life.

Third, not only does God require restitution and restoration, but He also created man to exercise dominion and to subdue the earth (Genesis 1:26-28). The redeemed man is restored to this calling in and by Christ. He is commanded to bring every thought into captivity to Christ (2 Corinthians 10:5), to carry the gospel to every creature and "to teach all nations" (Matthew 28:19). As Calvin pointed out, in reference to this latter verse, "The meaning amounts to this, that by proclaiming the gospel everywhere, they should bring *all nations* to the obedience of the faith."[4]

There is no conquest nor even life apart from regeneration, but the necessary and Scriptural goal of regeneration is to obey God by working to bring all things into captivity to Christ. Justification is by the grace of God through Christ; sanctification is by obedience to the law, not through the pagan pursuit of so-called charismatic manifestations. To separate the atonement and the law is to do violence to both. The law cannot be made a way of justification, as the Pharisees had done; Scripture pronounces the end to this false view of the law, and this misuse is declared to be a dead way, offering no hope. The Christian, moreover, is only *dead* to the law as an indictment and a death penalty against him. In Christ, he has died and is risen, and the law is now for him God's righteousness. God sent His Son, St. Paul declared, to condemn the old man on the cross, and He has placed us in the

---

4. John Calvin, *Commentary on a Harmony of the Evangelists, Matthew, Mark, and Luke*, vol. III, translated by William Pringle (Grand Rapids, MI: William B. Eerdmans, 1957), 383.

Spirit, and "in the law of the Spirit of life in Jesus Christ" (Romans 8:2) "that the righteousness of the law might be fulfilled in us" (Romans 8:4).

When our lives are founded upon the Rock, Jesus Christ, we are then like the house which the floods could not overwhelm (Matthew 7:24-27). God did not regard the law lightly: it cost Him the death of Jesus Christ. The law is serious in God's sight: grace and the law are alike aspects of His righteousness and of His glorious workings in our lives.

Because we are the people of grace, we are also the people of the law, and we find in grace and law the manifest righteousness of God.

For the ungodly, power means the ability to change others. For us, power means the Almighty One, whose power unto salvation, the resurrection of man from the death of sin, is set forth in the atoning work and the resurrection of Jesus Christ. His power is made available to the people of the faith when they *obey* His law-word. The Lord echoed His words to Moses in Deuteronomy 28 when He declared to Solomon, "If my people, which are called by my name, shall humble themselves, and pray, and seek my face, and turn from their wicked ways; then will I hear from heaven, and will forgive their sin, and will heal their land" (2 Chronicles 7:14).

The Collapse of Humanistic Power

In an important study of the modern era, Harvey Gross observes, "[w]e no longer have Heaven but we do have history."[1] It was in Hegel that this deification of history came into focus, and it was Hegel who wrote also of the duty of philosophy to establish "a new religion,"[2] and the form it took was one in which history was god, and Hegel was his prophet. The historical process was deified by Hegel as *Geist* or Spirit. As Findlay noted, "[a]s a philosopher, Hegel believes in no God and no absolute except one that is revealed and known in certain experiences of individual human beings, to those whose being it is essential to be so revealed and known."[3] This human incarnation of the absolute as history Hegel saw in his own day, in Napoleon. Since then, others have seen it in Hitler, Stalin, F. D. Roosevelt, and others. Hegel also saw the incarnation in science, and wrote to C. G. Zellman on January

---

[1.] Harvey Gross, *The Contrived Corridor, History and Fatality in Modern Literature* (Ann Arbor, MI: University of Michigan Press, 1971), 3.
[2.] Friedrich Hegel, *On Christianity, Early Theological Writings*, Introduction by Richard Kroner, translated by T.M. Knox (New York: Harper Torchbook, 1948), 38.
[3.] J.N. Findlay, *Hegel: A Re-examination* (New York: Collier Books, 1962), 353.

23, 1807, that "Science alone is the theodicy."[4] Marx and Lenin were later to combine this theodicy of science with the state to produce the infallible dictatorship of the scientific socialist state. This was a logical conclusion. Hegel had also said that "the perfect embodiment of Spirit assumes—the State."[5] In terms of this faith, that *God is history*, Khrushchev could tell the United States, "We shall bury you; History is on our side."

Thus, the conclusion of the modern era and its philosophy is a new religion and a new absolute power, *the sovereign state* as the incarnation and goal of History. Very few Christians caught the significance of this new religion. One who clearly did was the Catholic Conrad Von Boladen, whose writings were soon proscribed in his native Germany. In *The New God* (translated into English in 1872 by the Very Rev. Theodore Noethen), he made it clear that "the new State—God" was an absolute and jealous god bent on destroying Christianity and bringing all men into subjection to itself.

Within humanistic circles, a new atheism began to develop in the nineteenth century, atheism with respect to the god-state. The anarchists were the humanistic doubters of the god of humanism, and the anarchistic revolutionists began a death of god movement, a concerted and intensive effort to kill the new god, to strangle him in his infancy, as it were. The role of these anarchists as the great dissenters within the fold of humanism was not appreciated by the church, nor was it grasped. The anarchist, however, was still a man with hope: he believed that the natural goodness of man would lead to true order once the great evil environment of the state was removed. History as god would then reveal itself in the peace of autarchy.

One man went beyond the anarchists. As Harvey Gross points out, Nietzsche saw the end of historical existence, the death of the new state-god and of historical process.[6] In *Thus*

---

[4] Walter Kaufmann, *Hegel, Reinterpretation, Texts, and Commentary* (Garden City, NY: Doubleday, 1965), 318.

[5] G.W.F. Hegel, *Philosophy of History* (New York: Collier, 1901), 61.

[6] Gross, *op. cit.*, 11.

Spake Zarathustra, Nietzsche attacked two gods, the God of
Scripture, and the god of humanism, the historical state. He
described the state as "The New Idol" which roars, "[o]n earth
there is nothing greater than I: it is I who am the regulating
finger of God."[7]

Nietzsche's faith in *life* as the new hope of man steadily gave
way to a suicidal negation of the new and old gods, to a view
of the Superman as the great nay-sayer, the negater of all things
whose life is in essence a studied contempt for life, God, state,
and humanity, and an affirmation of what has been called evil
because it represents hostility and increasing opposition to all
that is called good, to all that is law and order. As Nietzsche
declared:

> "Man is evil"—so said to me for consolation, all the wisest
> ones. Ah, if only it be still true to-day! For the evil is man's
> best force.
>
> "Man must become better and eviler"—so do *I* teach. The
> evilest is necessary for the Superman's best.
>
> It may have been well for the preacher of the petty people
> to suffer and be burdened by men's sin. I, however, rejoice
> in great sin as my great *consolation.* —
>
> Such things, however, are not said for long ears.[8]

The Superman is one who sees that historical process is
vanity, and the ideals of men illusions, and so he attacks
unceasingly all hope in history or beyond history. This
Superman, of course, is Nietzsche himself, whose one ideal is
the projection of himself as the great Superman who is beyond
all faiths and all illusions. In *Ecce Homo*, Nietzsche declared:

> The very last thing I should promise to accomplish would
> be to "improve" mankind. I set up no new idols; I only
> want old idols to learn what it means to have feet of clay.
> To overthrow idols (the name I give to ideals) is very much
> more like my business. In proportion as we have invented

---

7. Friedrich Nietzsche, *Thus Spake Zarathustra*, in *The Philosophy of
Nietzsche* (New York: Modern Library, n.d.), 64.
8. *Ibid.*, 287; *Thus Spake Zarathustra*, in *ibid.*, 5.

an ideal world we have deprived reality of its value, its meaning, and its truth.... The "true world" and the "apparent world"—in plain English, the fictitious world and reality.... Hitherto the *lie* of the ideal has been the curse of reality; by means of it man's most basic instincts have become mendacious and false; so much so that those values have come to be worshipped which are most exactly antagonistic to the ones which would ensure man's prosperity, his future, and his great right to that future.[9]

Nietzsche declared total war on all things and predicted that his influence would lead to total war, "wars, whose like have never been seen on earth before. Politics on a grand scale will date from me."[10] Moreover, he declared, "[t]he sight of man now fatigues.—What is present-day Nihilism if it is not *that?*— We are tired of *man.*"[11] For Nietzsche, the old order of Assassins was "that order of free spirits *par excellence.*"[12] The true Superman is the absolute assassin of man.

As a result, Nietzsche held:

> Our first principles: no God: no purpose: limited energy. We will take good care to *avoid* thinking out and prescribing the necessary lines of thought for the lower orders.[13]

For Nietzsche, because all things pass away, they deserve to pass away, including man. As Gross saw so clearly, Nietzsche's "myth or Eternal Recurrence" was not a philosophy *of* history but "a philosophy *against* history."[14]

This new atheism, against history and its incarnation, the state, appears also, as Gross points out, in W.B. Yeats' poetry. *The Second Coming* depicts a grim future: anarchy becomes total, because there is now no center and focus to life, and bloody strife becomes the rule. Meanwhile, the "rough beast, its hour come round at last, Slouches towards Bethlehem to be

---

[9.] *Ibid.*, 6; *Ecce Homo*, in *ibid.*, Preface, 2.

[10.] *Ibid.*, 134; *Ecce Homo*, "Why I Am a Fatality," 1.

[11.] *Ibid.*, 26; *The Genealogy of Morals*, in *ibid.*, First Essay, 12.

[12.] *Ibid.*, 163; *The Genealogy of Morals*, Ascetic Ideals, 24.

[13.] Friedrich Nietzsche, *The Will to Power* (New York: Fredrick Publications, 1960), 99.

[14.] Gross, *op. cit.*, 13.

born." In *Supernatural Songs V*, "Ribh Considers Christian Love Insufficient," Yeats wrote:

> Why should I seek for love or study it?
> It is of God and passes human wit.
> I study hatred with great diligence,
> For that's a passion in my own control,
> A sort of besom that can clear the soul
> Of everything that is not mind or sense.[15]

What was an academic faith with Nietzsche and Yeats became, in the 1960s, an enacted creed with students everywhere, total hatred, suicidal causes for the sake of defeat, and a warfare against history. The new god, the state, was savagely attacked by the new atheism as the Establishment, as the incarnation of all evil.

In *Meru*, Yeats saw civilization's rule and peace as a product of "manifold illusion" and predicted the end of man, "his glory and his monuments."[16] The task of man, therefore, to use Andre Malraux's phrase, "is to *organize* the apocalypse."[17]

But to organize the apocalypse means less and less to usher in the Marxist utopia and more and more to bring forth total judgment and damnation on all things. Thus, even as humanistic man creates the totalitarian state, he wills at the same time its *Gotterdämmerung*, not only the twilight but also the death of his gods and all their power. History is denied in the name of apocalypse, and the humanistic apocalypse is total judgment and destruction, without any salvation.

[15.] *The Collected Poems of W.B. Yeats* (New York: Macmillan, 1962), 284.
[16.] *Ibid.*, 287.
[17.] Cited from *Man's Hope* by Gross, *op. cit.*, 137.

The Social Implications of Darwinism

1

Power From Below

In order to understand the social implications of Darwinism, it is necessary to recognize that the evolutionary hypothesis had deep roots in the preceding centuries, going back at least to the beginnings of modern philosophy. The idea of cultural evolution was given full-fledged formulation well before Darwin by the philosopher Hegel, and the idea was so fully a part of the culture of Darwin's day that more than one man was applying the concept to science by the mid-nineteenth century. In sociology, religion, history, and various other studies, the triumph of evolution had preceded Darwin. One might well say that the building had already been built: Darwin added the finishing touches and formally dedicated the edifice. With the structure completed (which did not preclude later alterations and developments), the scaffolding was quickly removed. Earlier formulations of the myth of evolution had been cautious: the exact form of the new structure had been somewhat blurred by the scaffolding, *i.e.*, the God-idea was utilized by some writers, and the sharpness of the break with Christian concepts denied, obscured, or minimized. After Darwin, the fortress was complete, and compromise was unnecessary.

For Darwin, man's very ideas and faith were biological products. As he told his cousin, "I look upon all human feelings as traceable to some germ in the animals."[1] Such a view reduces religion to pathology, and Darwin was unwilling to consider it seriously. He was bewildered by the reaction of many clergymen and theologians who were ready to see a 'higher' and 'nobler' Christianity arising out of evolutionary thought.[2] The difference between Darwinism and Christianity was in Charles Darwin's eyes too great for such a compromise or reconciliation.

Darwin was right. The triumph of Hegelian philosophy in Charles Darwin's theory marked a sharply different world and life view from that of Scripture. In the Bible, the determination of history, the creation of all things and the government of all things, is from God, from beyond history, from eternity. The Bible begins by declaring that "In the beginning God created the heavens and the earth" (Genesis 1:1). We are told, moreover, that "Through faith we understand that the worlds were framed by the word of God, so that things which are seen were not made of things which do appear" (Hebrews 11:3). Emphatically, the Bible declares that the determination of history is from beyond history, and the power that created and governs all things is from above history, above man and the universe.

Equally clearly, Darwinism holds to a radically different kind of origin, an accidental birth of the universe, its accidental development, and chance variations as the source of all things. Predestination is replaced by chance, and a universe of total purpose and meaning gives way to a mindless, meaningless accident. *As the motive force for all things, power from above has given way to power from below.*

It is impossible to underestimate the importance of this change. *Power* is inseparable from authority and religion. The people of Elijah's day, who had earlier bowed the knee to Baal,

---

[1] Gertrude Himmelfarb, *Darwin and the Darwinian Revolution* (Garden City, NY: Doubleday Anchor Books, 1962), 384.

[2] *Ibid.*, 394.

fell on their faces and said, "The LORD, he is God; the LORD, he is God" (1 Kings 18:39), when they saw Elijah's prayer miraculously answered. It was power that commanded them. If men believe that power in the universe comes from God, they will fear or worship God; if they believe that it comes from below, they will fear or worship that which is below.

As a result of the myth of evolution, a great cultural revolution has been in progress from before Hegel. Art has been a pioneer in this movement, sometimes formulating philosophy's direction before the philosophers themselves. The Age of Reason gave way to Romanticism, and mind gave way to feelings as the determinative force in man. The emotional life of man was held to have more vitality, because it represented the primitive, raw, and hence vital well-springs of being. Rousseau was an expression and voice of this belief, which infected politics and every other area of life. The idealization of the primitive man was an aspect of this new faith, and it soon followed that primitive acts and impulses were also a source of power. The quest was on for what Kenneth Burke called "grace from below." More than one scholar has seen the modern quest as one for a new kind of grace. According to Steiner, with the French Revolution, "[t]he great metaphor of renewal, of the creation, as by a second coming of secular grace, of a just, rational city for man, took on the urgent drama of concrete possibility."[3] The quest for secular grace involved, *first*, a destruction of the supposedly false, restraining force of Christianity, which had impeded man's free and natural self-expression. The old pagan ideals were revived; man was to find release in this "second coming of secular grace," a return to primitivism and an uninhibited expression of his every desire. This meant the ready exploration of the *abnormal*. As men had previously sought *holiness*, men now sought *sin*. This was the *second* aspect of the quest, the adoption of the abnormal and the primitive as the source of grace and power. Mario Praz documented this search

---

[3.] George Steiner, *In Bluebeard's Castle, Some Notes Towards the Redefinition of Culture* (New Haven, CT: Yale University Press, 1971).

at great length in his study, *The Romantic Agony*. Steiner describes it briefly in these words:

> Romantic ideals of love, notably the stress on incest, dramatize the belief that sexual extremism, the cultivation of the pathological, can restore personal existence to a full pitch of reality and somehow negate the gray world of middle-class fact.[4]

The world has seen a progressive cultivation by deliberate intent of the perverted and the primitive. It is not surprising, then, that politics and war have been brutalized, and that between 1914 and 1945, in Europe and Russia alone, some seventy million people have been killed by war, starvation, and massacre.[5] Since then, the pace of murder has only increased, especially as Asia has moved into the modern world and become better equipped to kill.

Third, by replacing power from above with power from below, *revelation has been replaced by experience*. Experience has become the new means of revelation, the new key to life and truth. One researcher in 1929 found that an important reason for adultery among women is the belief that without this experience, they will miss something in life.[6] This is even more true today.

The American poet Alan Seeger is a dramatic example of this fact. He is best known for one of the superior poems of World War I, in which he lost his life, "I Have a Rendezvous With Death." A young Harvard graduate, he went to France in 1913, and, when the war broke out a year later, he joined the French Foreign Legion and was killed in action at Belloy-en-Senterre in 1916. We are told by Wilkinson that "Alan Seeger, as everybody knows, went into the war with impetuous and generous gallantry, before this nation went into it, and for love

---

4. *Ibid.*, 21.
5. *Ibid.*, 30.
6. Lewis Joseph Sherrill, *Family and Church* (New York: Abingdon Press, 1937), 116f.

of France, the foster-mother of his spirit."[7] The truth is better stated by Seeger, who began his famous poem thus:

> I have a rendezvous with Death
> At some disputed barricade,
> When Spring comes back with rustling shade
> And apple-blossoms fill the air—
> I have a rendezvous with Death
> When Spring brings back blue days and fair.

In a letter to a friend almost four months before his death, Seeger stated the matter even more clearly:

> My interest in life was passion, my object to experience it in all rare and refined, in all intense and violent forms. The war having broken out, then, it was natural that I should have staked my life in learning what it alone could teach me. How could I have let millions of other men know an emotion that I remained ignorant of? Could not the least of them, then, talk about the thing that interested me most with more authority than I? You see, the course I have taken was inevitable. It is the less reason to lament if it lead me to destruction. The things one poignantly regrets are those which seem to us unnecessary, which, we think, might have been different. This is not my case. My being here is not an accident. It is the inevitable consequence, as you see, of a direction deliberately chosen.[8]

The quest for death as the ultimate experience is no less common today, but, at the moment, it takes on forms other than that of war.

In the same generation, Margaret Widdemer gave poetic voice to the same quest for experience as the new revelation. Her poem, "A Cyprian Woman," speaks of the peace a dead woman feels in her grave, having experienced all that a woman can:

> Under dusky laurel leaf,
> Scarlet leaf or rose,

---

7. Marguerite Wilkinson, *New Voices, An Introduction to Contemporary Poetry* (New York: Macmillan, 1928), 250.
8. *Letters and Diary of Alan Seeger* (New York: Charles Scribner's Sons, 1917), 186f.

> I lie prone who have known
> All a woman knows.

The poem concludes with the lines:

> I am glad, who have had
> All that life can tell.

Since then, of course, the quest has taken an energetic and determined course into the underworld of experience, drugs, perversion, and the occult.

This has meant, *fourth, the rise of magic, witchcraft, and occultism as means to the true source of power, and the revival of Satanism, power from below, as an article of faith and hope.* In the post-Darwinian world, faith in Satan is much more logical than faith in Jesus Christ.

Man needs power; he is helpless without it. If he denies that power can come from above, he will seek it in the world, or, in terms of the logic of evolution, he will seek it from below. The readiness with which modern "scientific" man, the product of a naturalistic philosophy of education, believes in occultism and Satanism should not surprise us. The only powers he recognizes as determinative in the development of the universe are subterranean and mindless, and the new idea of Satan is a more fearful one than Scripture presents. The new Satan is mindlessly perverse: he is the devil created in the image of Darwin's man.

Moreover, *fifth*, man, created in the image of God according to Scripture, has a different image according to Darwin. He is created in the image of a savage animal who stands and walks erectly but is still ruled by the old instincts of the pack.

Freud, who applied Darwinism to man, saw three basic instincts in man, by means of which he explained the whole life of man. Primitive man lived in a pack; the fathers possessed the mothers and daughters and drove out the mature sons. The sons banded together to kill the fathers and possess the mothers and daughters and to eat the fathers. The three basic drives of man are thus parricide, cannibalism, and incest. Instead of a man created in the image of God, in knowledge, righteousness, and holiness, with dominion over the creatures (Genesis 1:26-28; Colossians 3:10; Ephesians 4:24), we have modern man re-making himself after the image of an imaginary primitive man.[9] The consequences of this have been far-reaching.

We have had, for a century and a half, the control of education by the state and by evolutionary ideologues, Hegelian and Darwinian. The result has been the steady attrition of Christian faith and life, and the decline of effective Christian action. A system of education which is radically and totally governed by Hegelian and Darwinian assumptions has inescapable consequences for man. It leads to the quest for power from below, and to the radical debasement and degradation of man.

The rapid development of Christian schools since 1950 is the surest sign of a coming change in the character of civilization, of the end of humanism and its myth of evolution, and of a return to a Christian culture. More accurately, it means not a *return* to the past but the development of a *new* and vigorous Christian culture. Such a development is not possible without Christian schools.

---

9. See R.J. Rushdoony, *Freud* (Nutley, NJ: Presbyterian and Reformed Publishing Co., 1973).

2

The Conflict of Interests

We have seen some of the social implications of the modern world view as it expresses itself in Darwinism and the myth of evolution. All of the aspects cited have very serious consequences for education. There is still another basic factor that radically colors all of life and education, and which has substantially altered the world, namely, the idea of *conflict* as necessary, inescapable, and inevitable. In Darwinism, this idea of conflict is called *the struggle for survival*, and *natural selection*. In *The Descent of Man*, Darwin, among other things, had this to say about the matter:

> I have hitherto only considered the advancement of man from a semi-human condition to that of the modern savage. But some remarks on the action of natural selection on civilised nations may be worth adding. This subject has been ably discussed by Mr. W.R. Greg, and previously by Mr. Wallace and Mr. Galton. Most of my remarks are taken from these three authors. With savages, the weak in body or mind are soon eliminated: and those that survive commonly exhibit a vigorous state of health. We civilised men, on the other hand, do our utmost to check the process of elimination: we build asylums for the imbecile, the maimed, and the sick; we institute poor-laws;

137

and our medical men exert their utmost skills to save the life of every one to the last moment. There is reason to believe that vaccination has preserved thousands, who from a weak constitution would formerly have succumbed to small-pox. Thus the weak members of civilised societies propagate their kind. No one who has attended to the breeding of domestic animals will doubt that this must be highly injurious to the race of man. It is surprising how soon a want of care, or care wrongly directed, leads to the degeneration of a domestic race; but excepting in the case of man himself, hardly any one is so ignorant as to allow his worst animals to breed.[1]

For Darwin, social progress is thus a product of natural selection. We do not have space here to analyze the myth of the superior health of the savage which is a product of this idea, or the fact that the idea that "natural selection" is necessarily operative in "primitive" cultures is an illusion. Our concern is with the effects of this idea on our culture. Before considering these effects, we should also note that Darwin was aware of the offense of this idea to Christian morality, and he tried often to nullify that offense, to affirm the need for traditional virtues, and to retain some ethics in the face of his totally mindless universe.[2] He tried to save morality by positing social instincts which brought men together. However, according to natural selection, it was *might* which brought men together, the more powerful members of the pack governing and using the weaker. Carlyle, as a Hegelian like Darwin, was more consistent in applying this principle, and Darwin was horrified. Of Carlyle, Darwin wrote, "his views about slavery were revolting. In his eyes might was right."[3] As we have seen, Darwin had said, "I look upon all human feeling as traceable to some germ in the animals."[4] This view, however, had been

[1] Charles Darwin, *The Descent of Man* (Chicago: Encyclopaedia Britannica, 1952), 322.

[2] John C. Greene, *Darwin and the Modern World View* (Baton Rouge, LA: Louisiana State University Press, 1961), 98.

[3] Nora Barlow, editor, *The Autobiography of Charles Darwin 1809-1882* (New York: Harcourt, Brace, and Co., 1958), 113.

[4] Gertrude Himmelfarb, *Darwin and the Darwinian Revolution* (Garden City, NY: Doubleday Anchor Books, 1962), 384.

privately expressed to his cousin. Publicly, he did not dare dismiss all possibility of any morality. Victorian society did *not* want Christianity, but it did want some kind of traditional morality to protect against anarchy. Thus, as Darwin developed the idea of natural selection in *The Descent of Man*, he was careful to reassure his readers:

> Looking to future generations, there is no cause to fear that the social instincts will grow weaker, and we may expect that virtuous habits will grow stronger, becoming perhaps fixed by inheritance. In this case the struggle between our higher and lower impulses will be less severe, and virtue will be triumphant.[5]

How ready Darwin's age was to believe the myth is apparent in this passage, and in the fact that the entire edition of *On the Origin of Species* sold out on the day of publication, November 24, 1859. In the above passage, Darwin converted the idea of might and natural selection into a wonderful moral and social instinct. Then, in radical contradiction to his theory, he posited the inheritance of acquired characteristics, an idea that was often slipped into his theory.

Conflict could not be eliminated from Darwinism by these subterfuges, and the idea of conflict quickly became a part of society. It already had deep roots in the Hegelian doctrine of cultural evolution. The idea of *class conflict* was and is basic to socialism; this is why, among other things, Marx and Engels were overjoyed at the publication of *On the Origin of Species*. Once Darwin's premise of conflict became a scientific fact, socialism would become the inevitable form of society. Historic capitalism also underwent a radical change under the influence of Darwin and Spencer. Social Darwinism applied the idea of conflict and the survival of the fittest to the market-place, and the true free-market theory of *the harmony of interests* gave way to a socialistic premise of conflict which soon undercut capitalism.

---

5. Darwin, *op. cit.*, 319.

The idea of *the conflict of interests* was first proposed by the tempter in the Garden of Eden. God, he held, was concealing the true facts from man, lest man become a rival god. God was foisting an idea of *the harmony of interest* on man, so that man would be content to live in ignorance and continue in subservience to God. The universe, Satan's premise implied, is one of total conflict, with many gods possible, each striving against the other for total freedom. Such a theory means that the weak must fall, that the strong must seek greater strength, and, either by confrontation or guile, the would-be god must seek autonomous power and authority in all things.

The result of the tempter's thesis was, *first* of all, conflict between man and God; *second*, conflict between man and man; and, *third*, conflict within the soul of man.

The law of God and the redemptive work of Jesus Christ affirm, as against this, a different goal, the overcoming of the conflict of interests by, *first*, harmony between God and man through the atoning sacrifice of Jesus Christ; *second*, harmony between man and man by means of God's grace and in terms of His laws; and, *third*, peace in the soul of man by means of the Holy Spirit indwelling the redeemed.

Now, as we examine the school curricula, we can see a vast difference between the worldview of Darwinism and its theory of conflict, and the Bible and its doctrine of harmony. In the sciences, the conflict idea gives us not only the survival of the fittest, but also a view of the universe as a dead, hostile place, mindless, and alien to man. Man is an accident, as is the universe, and there is no meaning or purpose to anything; only the ugly conflict of man, with his will to survive, against a universe which is totally thoughtless of man. As against this, the Bible declares, in Psalm 19, that the God who is man's redeemer is the giver of the law and the creator of all nature, so that there is a perfect harmony in all things because God is perfect in all His ways:

> 1. The heavens declare the glory of God; and the firmament sheweth his handywork.

2. Day unto day uttereth speech, and night unto night sheweth knowledge.

3. There is no speech nor language, where their voice is not heard.

4. Their line is gone out through all the earth, and their words to the end of the world. In them hath he set a tabernacle for the sun.

5. Which is as a bridegroom coming out of his chamber, and rejoiceth as a strong man to run a race.

6. His going forth is from the end of the heavens, and his circuit unto the ends of it: and there is nothing hid from the heat thereof.

7. The law of the LORD is perfect, converting the soul: the testimony of the LORD is sure, making wise the simple.

8. The statutes of the LORD are right, rejoicing the heart: the commandment of the LORD is pure, enlightening the eyes.

9. The fear of the LORD is clean, enduring for ever: the judgments of the LORD are true and righteous altogether.

10. More to be desired are they than gold, yea, than much fine gold: sweeter also than honey and the honeycomb.

11. Moreover by them is thy servant warned: and in keeping of them there is great reward.

12. Who can understand his errors? cleanse thou me from secret faults.

13. Keep back thy servant also from presumptuous sins; let them not have dominion over me; then shall I be upright, and I shall be innocent from the great transgression.

14. Let the words of my mouth, and meditation of my heart, be acceptable in thy sight, O LORD, my strength, and my redeemer.

This is not a scientific account that the psalmist gives us, but it is still more accurate than the modern scientific view. Burtt gave a very telling account of the mechanical and cold universe that man began to see after Newton:

Newton's authority was squarely behind that view of the cosmos which saw in man a puny irrelevant spectator (so far as a being wholly imprisoned in a dark room can be called such) of the vast mathematical system whose regular motions according to mechanical principles constituted the world of nature. The gloriously romantic universe of Dante and Milton, that set no bounds to the imagination of man as it played over space and time, had now been swept away. Space was identified with the realm of geometry, time with the continuity of number. The world that people had thought themselves living in—a world rich with colour and sound, redolent with fragrance, filled with gladness, love and beauty, speaking everywhere of purposive harmony and creative ideals—was crowded now into minute corners in the brains of scattered organic beings. The really important world outside was a world hard, cold, colourless, silent and dead; a world of quantity, a world of mathematically computable motions in mechanical regularity. The world of quantities as immediately perceived by man became just a curious and quite minor effect of that infinite machine beyond. In Newton the Cartesian claim for serious philosophical consideration, finally overthrew Aristotelianism and became the predominant world-view of modern times.[6]

Cold as Newton's worldview was, there was still room in it for God as the great mathematician. In Darwin's worldview, there was only nature, red in tooth and claw, mindless and beset with total conflict in the struggle for survival. Darwin had grounds for believing in the harmony of interests because of his study of earthworms and their work, but he chose to accept the idea of the conflict of interests. The cold, dead, and hostile universe of Darwin is a myth. The world of Psalm 19 gives us the harmony of all things in and under God. So great is this harmony, that, as the psalmist declared, "Surely the wrath of man shall praise thee" (Psalm 76:10).

Contrary to Darwin, the socialists, and modern philosophy, there is no *metaphysical* conflict of interests in the universe; there is only an *ethical* conflict between covenant-breaking man and his God, but the sovereign God nullifies this conflict and makes it work together for good (Romans 8:28), and to His glory. The whole universe, and all things therein, move, Psalm 19 affirms, to glorify God: His purpose governs it

---

[6.] E.A. Burtt, *The Metaphysical Foundations of Modern Science* (New York, 1925), 236.

absolutely and gives harmony to all things in terms of His sovereign decree.

The textbooks in the sciences, as elsewhere, must thus be rewritten in terms of the Biblical doctrine of God as the Creator whose purpose establishes harmony and meaning. The Christian school cannot perpetuate the views of degenerate and metaphysically alien sciences.

Similarly, in economics and history, the conflict of interests theory leads to radical statism. It is assumed that there is no economic law inherent in God's universe and that man, through the state, must establish an order where none exists. The result is socialism. It is also taught that history is *class struggle* rather than an account of sin and man's rejection of God's harmony in favor of his own autonomy.

Again, in the teaching of grammar today, it is held that grammar is an arbitrary invention, and increasingly in the statist schools, any kind of expression is permitted, and, in fact, approved. To follow the rules is held to be repressive to the creative instinct. The comment of George Steiner on grammar is instructive at this point:

> An explicit grammar is an acceptance of order: it is a hierarchization, the more penetrating for being enforced so early in the individual life-span, of the forces and valuations prevailing in the body politic (the tonalities cognate). The sinews of Western speech closely enacted and, in turn, stabilized, carried forward, the power relations of the Western social order. Gender differentiations, temporal cuts, the rules governing prefix and suffix formations, the synapses and anatomy of a grammar—these are the *figura*, at once ostensive and deeply internalized, of the commerce between the sexes, between master and subject, between official history and utopian dream, in the corresponding speech community.[7]

Thus, while Steiner believes that "grammar is an acceptance of order," he believes that this order is relative to its culture. True,

---

[7.] George Steiner, *In Bluebeard's Castle, Some Notes Towards the Redefinition of Culture* (New Haven, CT: Yale University Press, 1971), 113.

anything in history is by that fact relative, but is it only relative? With this, the Christian cannot agree. The facts of time and relativity in time are God-created facts. *First*, all speech has *an inescapable time structure* because man lives in time. Again, *second*, all grammar or all speech has an *order* to convey the meaning, relationship, and sequence of things in time. *Third*, all speech, all words, are *propositional*: certain things are affirmed and delimited. Every word is a proposition, and every form of grammar is a propositional statement. *Fourth*, language and grammar are geared to *reality and communication*, and a lie or a falsehood defeats the function of language. *Fifth*, we must believe that language exists because God exists, and God, having created man in His image, has chosen to communicate with man, and to give man an infallible word. In Matthew 22:32 our Lord rests an important doctrine and its truth on the grammatical tense of God's word.

Because Darwinism teaches a conflict of interests, it is not surprising that we have what is evasively called "a generation gap," or, more accurately, a war between parents and children, teachers and pupils, the old and the young. We also have more racial conflict than the world has ever known.

In contrast, the Christian school, where faithful to its calling, brings harmony to the generations and between person and person, *not* in terms of the humanistic ideas of love, but in terms of the redemptive power of Jesus Christ. It is an imperative, therefore, that the Christian school curriculum work towards an entirely new kind of textbook and teaching, one furthering not the conflict of interests but the harmony of all interests under God.

3

On the Normality of Crime

"On the Normality of Crime" is a chapter heading from a most influential book by the sociologist Emile Durkheim, *The Rules of Sociological Method.* Durkheim's approach should not surprise us. According to the evolutionary worldview, there is no law of God handed down from above to declare what is good and evil, but only a world of chance below which is beyond good and evil, and in which, instead of moral law, we have random variations and developments. From the evolutionary point of view, the idea of the normal can thus mean one or another of, or a variation within, two categories. *First,* the normal can mean a statistical average. If fifty-one percent of the people in a society, or a higher percentage than are either married at the one "extreme" or celibate at the other, commit adultery, then adultery is normal behavior; it is possible, in terms of a statistical concept, to declare that in some societies chastity is abnormal. *Second,* the normal can mean that which occurs in nature. The Kinsey research report on sexual behavior rested on this premise. As a result, adultery, homosexuality, child molestation, and other forms of sexual perversion or deviation from God's law became natural and hence normal.

Durkheim's approach is essentially the second. He declares, "crime is normal because a society exempt from it is utterly impossible."[1] Society is offended by acts which go against its collective sentiment, Durkheim says. These acts can involve bad taste, wrong ideas, theft, murder, or a variety of offenses, whose punishment can vary from social displeasure to death. Crime is thus defined by Durkheim, as by all evolutionists, as an offense against a relativistic standard. The idea of what constitutes crime changes as society changes. The criminal is thus the man who disagrees with and acts contrary to social standards. (This definition could cover, in our evolutionary era, all evangelical Christians, as indeed it does in Marxist countries.) The "criminal character" is not a criminal because there is an absolute truth or law from which he departs but because he disagrees with society. In Durkheim's words,

> What confers this character upon them is not the intrinsic quality of a given act but that definition which the collective conscience lends them. If the collective conscience is stronger, if it has enough authority practically to suppress these divergences, it will also be more sensitive, more exacting; and, reacting against the slightest deviations with the energy it otherwise displays only against more considerable infractions, it will attribute to them the same gravity as formerly to crimes. In other words, it will designate them as criminal.[2]

Crime is thus a necessary part of society, because deviations from "the collective conscience" will always occur, but this does *not* mean that there is any evil inherent in crime or in the criminal. *The criminal thus is not a sinner but a social deviate.* His offense is purely relative: in one kind of society, he can be a criminal, and, in another, a hero. After all, Durkheim asserts, "it is no longer possible today to dispute the fact that law and morality vary from one social type to the next."[3] The Old

---

[1.] Emile Durkheim, *The Rules of Sociological Method* (Glencoe, IL: The Free Press, 1950), 65. Reprinted in Talcott Parsons, Edward Shils, K.D. Naegele, J.P. Pitts, editors, *Theories of Society, Foundations of Modern Sociological Theory*, vol. II (Glencoe, IL: The Free Press of Glencoe, 1961), 872.

[2.] *Theories of Society*, 873.

[3.] *Ibid.*

Testament prophets would not have disputed this either: they knew it only too well. Durkheim, however, refuses to acknowledge that the variations are sin, and that God's absolute law exists. For him, by definition, only the relative exists.

For Durkheim, the collective conscience is a constant factor; its content changes, but the collective intolerance of deviation is always there to inhibit the individual. At the same time, however,

> To make progress, individual originality must be able to express itself. In order that the originality of the idealist whose dreams transcend his century may find expression, it is necessary that the originality of the criminal, who is below the level of his time, shall also be possible. One does not occur without the other.
>
> Nor is this all. Aside from this indirect utility, it happens that crime itself plays a useful role in this evolution. Crime implies not only that the way remains open to necessary changes but that in certain cases it directly prepares these changes. Where crime exists, collective sentiments are sufficiently flexible to take on a new form, and crime sometimes helps to determine the form they will take. How many times, indeed, it is only an anticipation of future morality—a step toward what will be![4]

The criminal must thus be seen in a new light. He is not a totally unsociable being, nor is he an evil creature, but rather a social barometer and an evolutionary pioneer. His offense is not pathological, and this means that it does not require punishment, nor does it call for restitution. "If crime is not pathological at all, the object of punishment cannot be to cure it, and its true function must be sought elsewhere." Crime is a social not a moral fact. "The generality of phenomena must be taken as the criterion of their normality."[5] Here Durkheim tends to include the first definition of normality: crime is a *natural* fact, and it is also a *general* fact, so that it is doubly a normal aspect of society.

[4.] *Ibid.*, 874.
[5.] *Ibid.*, 874-875.

It follows, therefore, that what the criminal needs is not condemnation, but understanding. The social deviate has ostensibly been the object of unjust condemnation and should instead receive sympathy and sometimes appreciation.

Sigmund Freud, in a letter of 9 April 1935, rebuked a mother who was filled with horror and shame because her son was a homosexual. He stated, "[h]omosexuality is assuredly no advantage, but it is nothing to be ashamed of, no vice, no degradation; it cannot be classified as an illness; we consider it to be a variation of the sexual function, produced by a certain arrest of sexual development." The idea of a cure was ruled out by Freud: "What analysis can do for your son runs in a different line. If he is unhappy, neurotic, torn by conflicts, inhibited in his social life, analysis can bring him harmony, peace of mind, full efficiency, whether he remains homosexual or gets changed."[6]

Today, of course, Freud's view is bitterly attacked as reactionary because he regarded homosexuality as a form of arrested development. It is now held by many to be merely another form of natural sexual expression.

George B. Leonard, formerly a senior editor of *Look* Magazine, and also a vice-president of Esalen Institute of San Francisco and Big Sur, believes that evolution will work a great transformation in our total outlook. His vision is of "a society without criminals."

> To one whose field of existence has expanded to encompass more than his immediate surroundings, Eugene V. Deb's statement that "while there is a soul in prison, I am not free" becomes a matter, not just of thought and "practicality," but also of feeling and being. It becomes clear that people locked up in prisons, and animals in zoos, reflect something fearful locked up inside ourselves. Criminals are an essential part of our society and of each of us. Criminality is inextricably bound up with Civilization. If the Transformation involves

---

6. Ernst L. Freud, editor, *Letters of Sigmund Freud* (New York: Basic Books, 1960), 423f. See also R.J. Rushdoony, *Freud* (Nutley, NJ: Presbyterian and Reformed Publishing Co., 1973), 41f.

relinquishing what is criminal and freeing what is locked up within ourselves, it also involves emptying our prisons.[7]

Lest we miss the point and fail to see how far-reaching his ideas are, Leonard, who is advertised on the book-jacket as the father of four daughters, titles a key chapter, "Beyond Incest," although only three of forty-three pages deal with incest. He makes it clear, however, that he regards "the incest taboo" as "a good example of our blindness and confusion on sexual matters." Some cultures have practiced it, and he sees no valid social, genetic, or moral reason against it. He holds that "[t]he flowering of the Transformation will probably bring with it a progressive erosion of the incest taboo."[8]

The so-called underground press is busy today promoting every kind of illicit sex; and incest, for example, is strongly favored in many quarters. Their columns regularly defend incest and/or urge it as natural and healthy. In the 15 March 1974 issue of the *L.A. Star*, a woman writes in about her desire to commit incest with her fifteen year old son (whom she caught masturbating into her discarded panties). The position of Mrs. Robinson was in part this:

> I believe "What is natural is right." Our society believes what is unnatural is natural. Nature does not care that anyone is related to anyone else. That was started in this society because of birth defects. We have that anyway so I don't see that it is necessary to discriminate against relatives.
>
> What nature says is right our society says is against the law.[9]

Because cleanliness, like laws against incest, is a refusal to accept the natural world as normative, many hippies and "underground" papers ridiculed cleanliness and all distaste for bad odors. It is ironic that lack of cleanliness has reached such

---

[7.] George B. Leonard, *The Transformation, A Guide to the Inevitable Changes in Humankind* (New York: Delacorte Press, 1972), 178f.

[8.] *Ibid.*, 199f., 201.

[9.] *L.A. Star*, 15 March 1974, 4.

proportions among such people that their odors have become unendurable, by their own description. The *L.A. Star* devotes all of page 6 of the 15 March 1974, number to instructions in the use of toilet tissue (not used on principle by many), and the suggestion, "Change your underpants at least twice a week"! The totally natural world is thus not entirely tolerable even to its own champions.

Turning once again to the normality of crime, we can see something of the factors which, in recent years, have led college youths and liberals to regard rioting criminals as heroes. Having denied the idea of crime, they will naturally find allies in any circle bent on warfare against existing society, which still clings to the idea that some offenses are wrong.

How extensively the ideas of Durkheim and others have infected our culture can also be seen in the following illustration. On October 7, 1973, I spoke to at least 200 students at a major university; unlike most college and university groups I have spoken to, this was an entirely evangelical group. In discussing the doctrine of original sin, I asked how many had read Durkheim in the course of a classroom assignment. Almost all hands went up. I asked how many had read the chapter in *The Rules of Sociological Method* entitled, "On the Normality of Crime." Only one hand went up. I suggested that perhaps the reading of such a chapter would cause problems in their somewhat conservative state, and hence the bypassing of it by their professors. I then described the contents of that chapter and asked the students to raise their hands if to any measurable degree, the perspective and ideas of that chapter had been conveyed to them in the past. Again, almost all raised their hands. After the meeting, one student after another admitted to me that he or she (girls were more honest about admitting this) had been heavily brain-washed in their views of crime by this evolutionary approach.

Such an example makes it clear how radically different education is under evolutionary presuppositions and under Biblical presuppositions. We cannot underestimate the social damage caused by secular education. Neither can we permit churchmen to believe that it is other than morally wrong to turn their children and youths over to statist schools and secular universities. If the evolutionary mythology is both false and morally wrong, how much more wrong is it to turn our children over to the high priests of an evil faith?

4

The State as a Social Organization

The myth of evolution has led to a reduction of the idea of the state to that of a social organization, although some have called it an organism. Such a view has a seeming innocence: the state is, after all, a social organization, and to object to such a view seems parochial indeed. To define the state as a social organization, however, is like defining man as a largely hairless animal. There is a superficial truth to both statements, but, as they stand, they are lies. They do not define but rather distort and falsify that which they supposedly describe.

Man, in humanistic thought, has been described as a social animal, and the state has been accordingly described as a natural development of this aspect of this animal's nature. According to Scripture, however, man is a creature created in the image of God and called to act as God's vice-gerent, to rule the world under God and to make it God's Kingdom. Every aspect of man's life must be under God, and every institution must be an aspect of the Kingdom of God. Church, state, school, family, vocation, and all else must be made aspects of God's Kingdom and areas through which His word and law are set forth and obeyed. The state is thus far more than a *social* organization: it is and must be a *theological* organization. It is

153

either in the service of God, or it is against Him. It cannot be neutral. To call the state a social organization and to deny its theological frame of reference is to deform the state and to war against God.

Auguste Comte held that "the great theological dogma of the Fall of Man" was a prime source of error.[1] For him, it was necessary to abandon religion and philosophy for a purely scientific approach. This means denying the validity of any and every quest for *truth* in favor of a quest for *mythology*. In other words, it is not *meaning* which must govern society, but rather pragmatic technology.

Such a view places the state beyond good and evil. There is neither right nor wrong in anything that a state does, but only successful or unsuccessful technology and methodology. Stalin's forced collectivization of Soviet farmers or peasants in the early 1930s led to the death of 13 million people; in terms of his philosophy of science, this was not a moral wrong but merely an unsuccessful experiment, with no evil attached to its consequences.

When Hegelian and Darwinian doctrines led to the abandonment of all ideas of moral absolutes, of a transcendental law of God judging men and nations, law steadily began a transition from the idea of equity or justice to positive law, the fiat will of the state. Hallowell in 1943 documented this process whereby, in Nazi Germany, the point of tyranny had been reached. Several generations of liberal scholars, under the influence of a naturalistic and evolutionary concept of law, had stripped law of all reference to any idea of justice. God was no longer taken even remotely seriously as the author of law. In 1837, Dahimann had asked, "[m]ust I teach henceforward that the supreme principle of the State is that whatever pleases those in power is law? As a man of honor, I would cease to teach rather than sell to my audience

---

[1]. Talcott Parsons, Edward Shils, K.D. Naegele, J.P. Pitts, editors, *Theories of Society, Foundations of Modern Sociological Theory*, vol. I (Glencoe, IL: The Free Press of Glencoe, 1961), 126.

for truth that which is a lie and a deceit."[2] In less than a century, law of any kind was simply the enactment of the state, and no higher law was recognized. In the United States, Chief Justice Vinson, after World War II, declared, "[n]othing is more certain in modern society than the principle that there are no absolutes," and virtually every modern state acted on this same premise.

In terms of this, faith in God was not a vital factor, because it was unrelated to the problems of everyday life, and it did not govern the state and the world of man to any appreciable degree. The result was faith in *the state* and in the man leading the state, rather than faith in God. In Nazi Germany, this meant Hitler, in Soviet Russia, Stalin, and in Fascist Italy, Mussolini. In the United States, in the critical days after the inauguration of President Franklin Delano Roosevelt, idolization of him was such that Will Rogers happily wrote, "I don't know what additional authority Roosevelt may ask, but give it to him, even if it's to drown all the boy babies."[3] Men who have rejected God are more ready to worship the gods of the moment.

What does it mean to abandon the idea of truth, meaning, and moral absolutes? How can history then have direction? In the last century, Eccles, giving a naturalistic interpretation of sociology, had to say that, as water runs downhill, so, too, does man. "All movement, social as well as physical, is in the direction of least resistance, or of greatest traction."[4] As an evolutionist, Eccles believed that all this would somehow still lead to progress, but this conclusion was an affirmation of faith, not a product of his rational premise. The state, as Albert Jay Nock saw, has become the new church of man.[5]

[2.] John H. Hallowell, *The Decline of Liberalism as an Ideology, with Particular Reference to German Politico-Legal Thought* (Berkeley, CA: University of California Press, 1943), 7.

[3.] Cited by Amaury de Riencourt, *The Coming Caesars* (New York: Coward-McCann, 1957), 234.

[4.] R.J. Eccles, "The Study of Applied Sociology," in the symposium, *Man and the State, Studies in Applied Sociology* (New York: Appleton, 1892), 32.

[5.] Albert Jay Nock, *Our Enemy, the State* (New York: William Morrow, 1935).

The state is beyond good and evil, but it requires as the essential "good" obedience to itself! It dissolves all authority save its own, and it sees the life of man in essentially statist terms. The truly catholic and ecumenical "church" for modern man is the state: it includes all men without regard to race, creed, or color, and it is the one catholic institution in the modern world, or so it professes to be. Huizinga observed, in *The Shadow of Tomorrow* (1936), what a far-reaching claim the state makes:

> The position which the State professing its own amoral character arrogates to itself today is a very different one. As State it claims absolute autonomy and independence in respect to all moral standards. In so far as it allows the Church and religion, with their explicit and binding moral code, to carry on an existence of their own, their position is no longer one of freedom and equality but of subjection and compulsory allegiance to the doctrine of the State itself. It is clear that only those devoid of all religion will be able to embrace an ethical system of such glaring ambiguity.[6]

It has ceased, however, to be a "glaring ambiguity" to modern man. Schooled in humanism, he has come to see no reality beyond man and man's social organizations. This limited view of reality of the world of Darwin's children has come to some dead-end assumptions concerning the nature of things.

First, it is held that there is no such thing as absolute truth. All things are relativistic, and they are *relative to man*, and man's institutions, as the only tenable ultimate or absolute. God has been replaced by man and man's agencies as the new source of truth, as the criterion of good and evil, and as the standard for all judgment.

Second, theoretically, this faith in every man as his own god leads to anarchism, and this is also its practical application. As Marx recognized, however, anarchy, while logical, is also impractical and ruinous for man. Hence, communism was his

---

6. Johan Huizinga, "Regna Regnis Lupi?," in Waldo R. Browne, editor, *Leviathan in Crisis* (New York: Viking Press, 1946), 196.

pragmatic alternative, man's ultimacy turned over to an ultimate and absolute social organization. The state's remedy for the anarchism of a world without God is brute force, until such time as man can be remade into a creature of the beehive and see himself only as a social being. This will supposedly engender man's freedom and flowering.

Third, the scientific socialist state has no standard of good and evil to restrain it. Man becomes an experimental animal, to be used as the elite planners deem best. For some, this means electrodes in the brain as a means of social control. B.F. Skinner called for a world *Beyond Freedom and Dignity* (1971). From a creature of God, made in God's image, man is reduced to the role of a laboratory rat, a thing to be experimented with.

Fourth, in such a society, justice and freedom are what the state says they are, because there is no objective and transcendental frame of reference. There is only "society" as a scientific experiment. A statist school teacher once attacked me as misleading the people because I spoke of freedom. Her position was clear-cut: "In the modern world freedom is obsolete." In a world where evolutionary science is the only truth, the only way for man to remake himself and guide his evolution is by elite scientific planners assuming total control of man and society. In such an order, freedom is indeed obsolete. The state becomes the new god of man, and man becomes an experimental animal to be used to create a superman, or else he is discarded as waste material.

It is impossible for a Christian to give his consent to the evolutionist's doctrine of the state without sin. For the Christian, *first* of all, the state is an aspect of the Kingdom of God and has as much a duty to serve and obey the Lord as has the church. The Kingship of Jesus Christ is not limited to the church but includes the state, school, family, sciences, vocations, and all of life. Jesus Christ is the total savior: He is the savior of man, and of every institution of man. Without God, the state soon becomes, as St. Augustine pointed out in *The City of God*, simply another band of robbers. The state is not the church, but it is nonetheless Christian in its calling, and the requirements made of it are as exacting before God.

This means, *second*, that the state is essentially a religious institution rather than a social institution. Its present form is colored by the fact of the Fall, but, before the Fall, man lived in the Kingdom or State of God, and under God's Kingship.

Third, the Bible declares that the state is God's ministry of justice (Romans 13:1-7), and it must thus function primarily in terms of the word of God rather than the will of man. The state is a theological organization. Like the church, it can be an apostate ministry, but it is still by its ordination a theocentric institution.

Fourth, since the members and/or subjects of the state are creatures made in the image of God, the state can never regard them in any but theological terms, to be dealt with in terms of God's law, and to be kept in obedience to God's laws for society.

If the state is not godly, it will sooner or later wage war against God by attacking His people. There is and can be no neutrality. As a result, the mythology of evolution, as it comes to focus in the doctrine of the state, is a major threat to the future of Christ's people. It is necessary, therefore, to replace the myth with the doctrine of creation, and to create a Christian state and society, or else be destroyed by the humanistic state.

5

The Family

The Darwinian perspective has done particular damage to the family. Darwin's premise of *the conflict of interests* was rigorously applied to the idea of the family. *The Descent of Man* (1871) is divided into three parts: Part One, The Descent or Origin of Man; Part Two, Sexual Selection; Part Three, Sexual Selection in Relation to Man and Conclusion. In the last section, the thesis of Darwin's entire theory is formulated as a law, "The Law of Battle." As with the gorillas, Darwin held, "the law of battle had prevailed with man during the early stages of his development." Man's physical development was in terms of battle, the necessity to do battle with other males in order to possess the females. His canine and other teeth receded to a less important role only as man gradually became erect and "used his hands and arms for fighting with sticks and stones."[1] This continual necessity for battle on the part of man has enabled him, since the evolutionary mechanism is the struggle for survival and natural selection in terms of it, to develop greater strength than and a mind superior to women,

---

[1.] Charles Darwin, *The Descent of Man* (Chicago: Encyclopaedia Britannica, 1952), 565.

Darwin held.[2] There are other factors that enter into natural selection, but they are allied to or feed the law of battle.

In all of this, there is no morality in any historical Christian sense. For Darwin, "the moral sense" is an evolutionary product. As he summarized it:

> ...the moral sense follows, firstly, from the enduring and ever-present nature of the social instincts; secondly, from man's appreciation of the approbation and disapprobation of his fellows; and thirdly, from the high activity of his mental faculties, with past impressions extremely vivid; and in these latter respects he differs from the lower animals. Owing to this condition of mind, man cannot avoid looking both backwards and forwards, and comparing past impressions. Hence after some temporary desire or passion has mastered his social instincts, he reflects and compares the now weakened impression of such past impulses with the ever-present social instincts; and he then feels that sense of dissatisfaction which all unsatisfied instincts leave behind them, he therefore resolves to act differently for the future,—and this is conscience. Any instinct, permanently stronger or more enduring than another, gives rise to a feeling which we express by saying that it ought to be obeyed. A pointer dog, if able to reflect on his past conduct, would say to himself, I ought (as indeed we say of him) to have pointed at that hare and not have yielded to the passing temptation of hunting it.[3]

Conscience thus has no God-centered, theological and moral content; it has a purely social content and is hence essentially amoral. Moreover, since the law of battle is basic to life, *battle replaces morality* with regard to sex and the family. A valid complaint of the women's liberation movement is that woman has been reduced to a sexual object, used by men, but not respected or loved. The feminist indictment of the pin-up picture, and the theatrical world associated with it, is that it is "the packaging of rape." In both erotic imagination and in action, the woman is treated as an object of rape, *i.e.*, a battle-

---

2. *Ibid.*, 566f.
3. *Ibid.*, 592.

prize.[4] Because the women's liberation movement is so heavily governed by anti-Christian elements, it has often made the Bible and patriarchal attitudes its target of attack when its true enemy is evolutionary faith and its warfare society. Darwin gave sex a triply powerful position. *First,* sexual selection is basic to the evolutionary process, so that sex is seen as determinative in relation to man's advance, his nature, and his intelligence. Even more than Freud was credited with doing, Darwin sexualized the philosophy of modern man. *Second,* by seeing sexual selection and evolution in terms of "the law of battle," Darwin reduced life to conflict, and, even more, to sexual conflict, so that a radically disintegrative force was unleashed on the modern world by Darwinism. *Third,* for Darwin the God-idea was irrelevant and meaningless, and sex replaces God in Darwin as the determinative force in history. As Darwin wrote:

> The belief in God has often been advanced as not only the greatest, but the most complete of all the distinctions between man and the lower animals. It is, however, impossible, as we have seen, to maintain that this belief is innate or instinctive in man. On the other hand a belief in all-pervading spiritual agencies seems to be universal; and apparently follows from a considerable advance in man's reason, and from a still greater advance in his faculties of imagination, curiosity and wonder. I am aware that the assumed instinctive belief in God has been used by many persons as an argument for His existence. But this is a rash argument, as we should thus be compelled to believe in the existence of many cruel and malignant spirits, only a little more powerful than man; for the belief in them is far more general than in a beneficent Deity. The idea of a universal and beneficent Creator does not seem to arise in the mind of man, until he has been elevated by long-continued culture.

> He who believes in the advancement of man from some low organised form, will naturally ask how does this bear

---

[4.] Joan Nicholson, "The Packaging of Rape: A Feminist Indictment," fore-word to Mark Gabor, *The Pin-Up, A Modest History* (New York: University Books, 1972), 9-12.

on the belief in the immortality of the soul. The barbarous races of man, as Sir J. Lubbock has shewn, possess no clear belief of this kind, but arguments derived from the primeval beliefs of savages are, as we have just seen, of little or no avail. Few persons feel any anxiety from the impossibility of determining at what precise period in the development of the individual, from the first trace of a minute germinal vesicle, man becomes an immortal being; and there is no greater cause for anxiety because the period cannot possibly be determined in the gradually ascending organic scale....

Sexual selection has been treated at great length in this work; for, as I have attempted to shew, it has played an important part in the history of the organic world.[5]

How thoroughly Darwinian modern education and thought has become is apparent from any textbook, as well as from contemporary popular thought. Thus, Barnes's textbook, in discussing "Marriage and the Family in Contemporary Society," began with a discussion of "our Simian heritage."[6] Barnes was insistent that we cannot read our modern Christian ideas back into the nature of man, but he was equally insistent that the imaginary reconstructions of "primitive" man by Darwin and others had to be read into modern man! The family, he held, is declining as a social institution. The idea that it must always remain, or else remain essentially unchanged, had no validity for Barnes and others. Women's bondage to "an unpleasant and oppressive home environment" could not long exist. Social evolution was progressively taking man away from the idea of the family as a necessary institution. He conceded, however, that for the foreseeable future, the family would continue, although "[u]ndoubtedly readjusted in terms of social rationality."

A few years after Barnes, many were ready to maintain that we are building a new society in which both sex and child-rearing are separated from marriage. Some have denied that

---

[5.] Darwin, *op. cit.*, 593.
[6.] Harry Elmer Barnes, *Social Institutions in an Era of World Upheaval* (New York: Prentice-Hall, 1942), 601 ff.

parents are necessary to child-rearing, and the Israeli kibbutzim have been cited as proof for this thesis by Bruno Bettelheim.[7] Others have held that Christian ideas of morality have no objective validity.[8] The legalization of abortion has been a major step in the forwarding of these new ideas, and an example of the conflict view of Darwin: now the mother wages war against her unborn babe.

As against these conflict ideas of human sexuality, the Bible makes it clear that God created man male and female, to live together in harmony in the service of God. Family law is central to Biblical law, because the family is the basic institution of human society.[9] Justinian made "the Christian way of life" basic to the law. Zimmerman has summarized the basic Christian sex reforms of the Code of Justinian:

1. Only heterosex relations in marriage were made publicly allowable. All other forms of sex acts were classified as objectionable, non-human (mammalian, bestial, sinful, criminal), and as punishable.

2. This classification of "other forms" of sex as "objectionable" was applied to every social class, without regard to rank, economic condition, or occupation....

3. Sex activities were made punishable by physical means such as castigation, imprisonment, and banishment....

4. Contracts involving non-family sex activities as repayment for support or gifts were made illegal. They no longer became a defence in law but made the contractor an accessory to an illegal act....

5. These acts were not taken alone but as part of a wider movement to make the family the defined public way of life and status. Negative movements against extra

---

[7.] Bruno Bettelheim, "Does Communal Education Work? The Case of the Kibbutz," in Edwin M. Schur, editor, *The Family and the Sexual Revolution* (Bloomington, IN: Indiana University Press, 1964), 292-307.

[8.] See, in Schur's study, the essays in Part One, by Kinsey, Ellis, and others, on "Changing Sex Standards."

[9.] See R.J. Rushdoony, *The Institutes of Biblical Law* (Nutley, NJ: The Craig Press, 1974).

family sex were taken as part of a positive movement to promote universal familism.[10]

What these reforms accomplished was a major legal and cultural revolution. The history of Western civilization cannot be understood apart from them. Some of the central aspects can be cited. *First* of all, the Bible clearly gives the family custody of the children. This seems so natural and obvious a fact that we fail to realize how important it is. Control of children is basic to any control of the future. The reason why state control of education has been instituted in the modern era is precisely to prevent undue control of children by the family and the church, and to change society by attaching the children to the state rather than to parents and the church. Statist education is a form of warfare against the family (and against religion). Its purpose is to govern the child by giving him a statist rather than familistic orientation. The state school is an enemy of the family and of the church, and it is a weapon of statism.

Second, after children, who are the human future of society, control of property is next most important in the control of society. Here, also, the Bible ties property firmly to the family. The Biblical laws of inheritance prevent the disinheritance of a godly son (Deuteronomy 21:15-17); and an ungodly son could not be an heir but had to be denounced to the authorities (Deuteronomy 21:18-21). Property could not be alienated from the legitimate wife and her children: it was her dowered right. An illegitimate child thus could not be made a secret heir. The legal control of property by the legal family made the family the most powerful institution in society. A *third* aspect implicit in the second and already referred to is inheritance: the family not only controls the children and property, it also controls inheritance and thereby has great power over both children and the property.

Fourth, education in the Bible is controlled by the family. Parents are to "bring them up in the nurture and admonition

---

10. Carle C. Zimmerman, in Carle C. Zimmerman and Lucius F. Cervantes, *Marriage and the Family* (Chicago: Henry Regnery, 1956), 61f.

of the Lord" (Ephesians 6:4). Parents are inseparably morally linked to the education of their children (Proverbs 4:1-2, etc.). The separation of education from parental control and/or decision is thus a major attack on Christianity.

The modern anti-Christian, post-Darwinian state is hostile, *first*, to the family's custody of the children. In one form or another, it is steadily infringing on parental authority. *Second*, the progressive expropriation and/or control of property is under way, transferring ownership and/or control to the state. *Third*, education has been made an area of major statist concern, and, in some parts of the world, parents have been denied the right to educate their children or to have Christian schools. *Fourth*, inheritance has been taxed, and, by means of inheritance laws, the state has made itself the main or first-born heir of every family.

It is thus clear how serious the social implications of Darwinism are. To survive and overcome, Christianity must not only deny the myth of evolution, but it must also attack statism, establish Christian schools, and firmly root the Christian family in Jesus Christ and Biblical law.

Scripture Index

Index

The Author

Rousas John Rushdoony (1916-2001) was a well-known American scholar, writer, and author of over thirty books. He held B.A. and M.A. degrees from the University of California and received his theological training at the Pacific School of Religion. An ordained minister, he worked as a missionary among Paiute and Shoshone Indians as well as a pastor to two California churches. He founded the Chalcedon Foundation, an educational organization devoted to research, publishing, and cogent communication of a distinctively Christian scholarship to the world at large. His writing in the *Chalcedon Report* and his numerous books spawned a generation of believers active in reconstructing the world to the glory of Jesus Christ. He resided in Vallecito, California until his death, where he engaged in research, lecturing, and assisting others in developing programs to put the Christian Faith into action.

The Ministry of Chalcedon

CHALCEDON (kal•see•don) is a Christian educational organization devoted exclusively to research, publishing, and cogent communication of a distinctively Christian scholarship to the world at large. It makes available a variety of services and programs, all geared to the needs of interested ministers, scholars, and laymen who understand the propositions that Jesus Christ speaks to the mind as well as the heart, and that His claims extend beyond the narrow confines of the various institutional churches. We exist in order to support the efforts of all orthodox denominations and churches. Chalcedon derives its name from the great ecclesiastical Council of Chalcedon (A.D. 451), which produced the crucial Christological definition: "Therefore, following the holy Fathers, we all with one accord teach men to acknowledge one and the same Son, our Lord Jesus Christ, at once complete in Godhead and complete in manhood, truly God and truly man...." This formula directly challenges every false claim of divinity by any human institution: state, church, cult, school, or human assembly. Christ alone is both God and man, the unique link between heaven and earth. All human power is therefore derivative: Christ alone can announce that "All power is given unto me in heaven and in earth" (Matthew 28:18). Historically, the Chalcedonian creed is therefore the foundation of Western liberty, for it sets limits on all authoritarian human institutions by acknowledging the validity of the claims of the One who is the source of true human freedom (Galatians 5:1).

The *Chalcedon Report* is published monthly and is sent to all who request it. All gifts to Chalcedon are tax deductible.

Chalcedon
Box 158
Vallecito, CA 95251 U.S.A.
www.chalcedon.edu

Printed in the United States
201945BV00003B/1-156/A

9 781879 998308